somos así 2

Teacher's Edition

Somos así 2

Teacher's Edition Writers

James F. Funston
John F. Wilhite

EMC Publishing, Saint Paul, Minnesota

ISBN 0-8219-0994-0

Published by EMC Publishing
300 York Avenue
St. Paul, Minnesota 55101

Printed in the United States of America
  2 3 4 5 6 7 8 9 10 XXX 99 98 97 96 95

CONTENTS

SCOPE AND SEQUENCE CHART

Introducción		
<ul><li>Seeking and providing personal information</li><li>Talking about everyday activities</li><li>Describing the weather</li><li>Indicating a length of time</li><li>Talking about family and friends</li><li>Using the numbers 0- 999,999</li><li>Talking about dates and special days</li><li>Telling time</li></ul>		<ul><li>Talking about the future</li><li>Referring to what has just happened</li><li>Comparing quantity, quality, age and size</li><li>Discussing schedules</li><li>Stating what is happening right now</li><li>Talking about the past</li></ul>

	Readings	Notes	Grammar
Lección A	Me llamo Francisco Dragonetti Todos somos diferentes	El negativo con *no* Hablando del tiempo ¿Cuánto tiempo hace que...?	Los cognados El presente del indicativo I El presente del indicativo II
Lección B	Soy de México, D.F. Los parientes de Carmen María En la casa de Carmen María	La quinceañera Conectando frases con *que*	
Lección C	De compras en el supermercado	El presente para hablar del futuro El comparativo y el superlativo: un poco más El comparativo y el superlativo (continuación)	*Acabar de/ir a* + infinitivo El comparativo y el superlativo
Lección D	Estoy estudiando ahora, pero....		El presente progresivo La palabra *a*
Lección E	¿Qué hiciste el verano pasado?		El pretérito Más sobre el pretérito Afirmativos y negativos
Lección F	¿Me pueden ayudar?	Más sobre el complemento directo	El complemento directo El complemento indirecto Los dos complementos

Capítulo 1
La vida diaria

- Talking about everyday activities
- Expressing annoyance
- Seeking and providing personal information
- Discussing personal grooming
- Comparing and contrasting
- Recognizing and identifying Hispanic influence in the United States

- Stating when things are done
- Expressing past actions and events
- Identifying items in a bathroom
- Pointing something out
- Writing about everyday activities
- Discussing health
- Giving and taking instructions
- Identifying parts of the body

	Readings	Notes	Grammar
Lección 1	En Lapaz, pero no en paz El baño	Singular a plural Lugares geográficos con nombres en español La vida diaria Los verbos reflexivos: un poco más El artículo definido con verbos reflexivos El pretérito de los verbos reflexivos Las tres comidas	Los verbos reflexivos La palabra *se* Los adjetivos demostrativos Los pronombres demostrativos
Lección 2	En la oficina de la doctora Pino El cuerpo Una cita con el médico	*Pescar* Aquí se habla español ¿Qué oyes en la oficina del médico?; ¿qué puedes contestar? Más sobre los verbos reflexivos Verbos parecidos	Otras construcciones reflexivas Las preposiciones Los verbos después de las preposiciones
Lectura	¡Ay, Miguel!		

Capítulo 2 La ciudad	• Asking for and giving directions • Identifying places in the city • Discussing what is sold in specific stores • Telling someone what to do • Ordering from a menu in a restaurant	• Advising and suggesting • Discussing who and what people know • Talking about everyday activities • Telling others what not to do • Identifying parts of a car • Advising others in writing

	Readings	Notes	Grammar
Lección 3	En el centro En el centro (continuación) En un restaurante en la ciudad	Las tiendas con -ería México Las comidas nacionales Los cambios ortográficos	El mandato afirmativo informal El mandato afirmativo formal y el mandato plural El mandato con nosotros/as
Lección 4	En el barrio En casa de David En la exhibición de coches Las señales de tráfico	Los puntos cardinales México hoy Otros verbos como conocer El mandato negativo: un poco más	Los verbos conocer y saber El mandato negativo: un poco más
Lectura	¡Conozca México!		

Capítulo 3
¿Qué hacías?

- Seeking and providing personal information
- Describing in the past
- Talking about activities at a special event
- Identifying animals
- Expressing quantities
- Providing background information about the past
- Indicating past intentions
- Discussing nationality
- Adding emphasis to a description
- Recognizing and expressing size
- Stating possession
- Identifying sounds that animals make

	Readings	Notes	Grammar
Lección 5	En el parque de atracciones En el jardín zoológico	El Salvador Los usos del imperfecto ¿Qué es *América*? ¿Los nombres de animales o de personas? Los usos del imperfecto: un poco más *Más de....* ¿Cuál es tu nacionalidad?	El imperfecto de los verbos regulares El imperfecto de los verbos *ser, ir* y *ver* *Ser* vs. *estar*
Lección 6	En el circo En la finca ¿Qué dicen los animales?	Honduras ¿Qué hacen algunos de los animales? Los pronombres posesivos *Lo* con adjetivos/adverbios ¡Qué toro tan grande!	¡Buenísimo/a! *-ito* e *-ita* Los adjetivos y su posición Los adjetivos como sustantivos Los adjetivos posesivos: formas largas
Lectura	¡El gran Circo de los Hermanos Suárez!		

Capítulo 4 **¿Te acuerdas?**	• Talking about what someone remembers • Seeking and providing personal information • Describing clothing • Reporting past actions and events • Talking about everyday activities • Identifying foods • Using metric weights and measurements	• Reading and ordering from a menu • Writing about the past • Expressing opinions • Asking for advice • Stating what was happening at a specific time • Describing how something was done • Expressing length of time • Discussing food preparations

	Readings	Notes	Grammar
Lección 7	Estábamos en el supermercado ¿Por qué te ríes? El menú	Cuba El pretérito de conocer *Hay, había* o *hubo* El sistema métrico	El pretérito El pretérito y el imperfecto El presente de los verbos *reír* y *freír* Más verbos irregulares en el pretérito
Lección 8	El vestido para la cena El vestido para la cena (continuación) La cena La cena (continuación)	El Caribe El progresivo: un poco más *Lo:* un poco más	El imperfecto progresivo Los adverbios terminados en *-mente* Hace (+ *time*) que Hacía (+ *time*) que
Lectura	El Caribe		

Capítulo 5
Hogar, dulce hogar

- Telling someone what to do
- Reporting what others say
- Stating wishes and preferences
- Talking about everyday activities
- Talking about family
- Making a request
- Advising and suggesting
- Describing a household
- Expressing uncertainty
- Expressing doubt
- Expressing emotion
- Stating hopes
- Stating an opinion
- Discussing time

	Readings	Notes	Grammar
Lección 9	En la casa de Ramiro En la casa de Ramiro (continuación) Cosas por hacer Cosas por hacer (continuación) En el hogar	¿Qué recuerdas? Bolivia El subjuntivo con mandatos indirectos Los miembros de la familia: un poco más El subjuntivo con mandatos indirectos: un poco más Verbos de causa sin el subjuntivo La arquitectura hispana	El subjuntivo El subjuntivo con mandatos indirectos: *decir* y *querer* Verbos irregulares en el subjuntivo
Lección 10	Tienes que regresar temprano El cumpleaños de la abuela Algunos aparatos del hogar	Los países bolivarianos Otros verbos de emoción El subjuntivo con expresiones impersonales	El subjuntivo con verbos de emoción y duda El subjuntivo en cláusulas adverbiales El subjuntivo en cláusulas adjetivales
Lectura	La familia hispana		

Capítulo 6
¿Qué ha
pasado?
	• Expressing events in the past
	• Talking about the news
	• Discussing what has happened
	• Discussing a television broadcast
	• Talking about everyday activities
	• Describing people and objects
	• Writing about what someone
	  has done
		• Identifying sections of
		  newspapers and magazines
		• Relating two events in the past
		• Discussing a radio broadcast
		• Talking about soccer
		• Adding emphasis to a description
		• Expressing wishes

	Readings	Notes	Grammar

Lección 11	¿Qué ha pasado?
	¿Qué ha pasado?
	  (continuación)
	Los programas de la
	  televisión
	Los programas de la
	  televisión
	  (continuación)
		El Uruguay
		¿Qué ha pasado en las
		  noticias?
		Participios pasivos
		  irregulares
		El pretérito perfecto: los
		  verbos reflexivos
		El participio pasivo como
		  adjetivo
			El pretérito perfecto y
			  el participio pasivo

Lección 12	Yo había visto el periódico
	Las noticias se escuchan
	  por Radio Nacional
	El partido de fútbol
		En los periódicos y en las
		  revistas
		Paraguay
		Los prefijos
		El fútbol: un poco más
			El pretérito
			  pluscuamperfecto
			La voz pasiva
			La voz pasiva: un poco
			  más

Lectura	Infancia		

Capítulo 7
Haciendo planes

- Seeking and providing personal information
- Planning vacations
- Talking about the future
- Expressing emotion
- Talking about everyday activities
- Expressing uncertainty or probability
- Making travel and lodging arrangements
- Identifying people and items associated with travel
- Stating wishes and preferences
- Talking about schedules
- Using the twenty-four-hour clock
- Expressing logical conclusions
- Writing about hopes and dreams

	Readings	Notes	Grammar
Lección 13	¿Adónde irás de vacaciones? ¿Adónde irás de vacaciones? (continuación) ¿Saldremos temprano? En la agencia de viajes	Un domingo por la tarde La tortilla española El futuro de probabilidad El futuro: los verbos reflexivos	El futuro con *ir a* El futuro El futuro de los verbos irregulares
Lección 14	En el aeropuerto En el avión Al hotel En la recepción	La hora en algunos horarios España El condicional de los verbos irregulares ¿A qué hora? La diversidad cultural española Los hoteles El condicional de probabilidad	El condicional
Lectura	Lázaro cuenta su vida y de quién fue hijo		

Capítulo 8
Sueños y aspiraciones

- Discussing the future
- Expressing uncertainty
- Talking about hopes and dreams
- Seeking and providing information about careers
- Expressing events in the past
- Relating two events in the past

- Expressing doubt
- Advising and suggesting
- Stating wishes and preferences
- Expressing emotion
- Identifying and locating some countries
- Writing about the future

	Readings	Notes	Grammar
Lección 15	Espero que hayas decidido qué estudiar Los empleos Una amiga por correspondencia	Los empleos: un poco más	Usos de haber El pretérito perfecto del subjuntivo Más sobre el subjuntivo
Lección 16	Mi gran sueño El lenguaje del cuerpo El mundo	¿Adónde te gustaría viajar?; algunos países del mundo Para ser más natural	El futuro El subjuntivo: un resumen
Lectura	Lázaro cuenta su vida y de quién fue hijo (continuación)		

INTRODUCTION

Somos así is a practical, proficiency-oriented three-level Spanish language program that addresses the needs of students with varied learning styles. A principal goal of the program is to enable students to become capable of creative self-expression in authentic Spanish by providing teachers with a comprehensive and well-articulated program of instruction.

The series' textbooks and accompanying ancillaries evolved from a national survey of concerned foreign language educators, extensive discussions with experienced Spanish teachers and research on the application of state-of-the-art methods in foreign language teaching. The result of this effort is a practical step-by-step instructional program that interrelates and presents culture, grammar and vocabulary in a communicative manner, thus enabling students to understand and use authentic Spanish. With *Somos así*, students will enjoy using Spanish while becoming familiar with the culture of the various Spanish-speaking parts of the world.

Somos así 1 presented interesting new material in a visually appealing manner. These new concepts and skills are then spiraled throughout the rest of the series in *Somos así 2* and *Somos así 3*. This careful articulation from one chapter to the next, and from one level of the program to the next, is central to the methodology of the program. The systematic review, reinforcement and expansion in succeeding lessons of previously studied functions, vocabulary and structures is required to help students remember and connect familiar subject matter with new concepts and skills as they are introduced. A specific example of this can be readily observed in the review lesson entitled *Repaso,* which appears at the end of every numbered *Capítulo* of the *Somos así* program. Teachers may assign activities from the section to single students, to small groups or to the entire class, based upon student needs. The *Repaso* provides subsequent opportunities for students to use what they already have learned and culminates in an activity entitled *A crear* that encourages unrestricted self-expression.

Somos así provides a map for learning that empowers students to learn to comprehend spoken Spanish, speak, read and write, and to do so in a culturally authentic manner. Varied dialogs and readings (such as collages, letters, recipes, signs and articles from magazines and newspapers) on diverse topics will stimulate students to look beyond the classroom at real life in the Spanish-speaking world. Clear and comprehensive explanations of grammar that will guide students to understand and use Spanish with increasing accuracy appear after the structures already have occurred in realistic and natural settings. Interesting cultural, linguistic and paralinguistic notes appear throughout the textbook in the section *A propósito*. Activities are both creative and communicative, allowing the student to use Spanish in meaningful, everyday circumstances. In addition, the textbook provides a visual context for learning through abundant text-related photographs and illustrations.

The accompanying components of the series, which are described in this front section of the Teacher's Edition, have been carefully designed and written to provide instructors with an effective, flexible and manageable program for teaching students to communicate in Spanish. Whether an instructor requires additional writing practice, a listening comprehension activity, video, computer software or some other means of addressing student needs, materials for tailoring lesson plans are available to reinforce, recycle and expand upon the textbook content, thus allowing the teacher to decide which components and activities to use on a daily basis.

Perhaps the greatest challenge that educators face today is the need to reach a large number of students, each with individual interests and learning styles. A comprehensive, flexible instructional program allows educators and students to meet the challenge together. *Somos así* is our response to the need to provide practical, realistic and interesting teaching materials that appeal to both teachers and students alike.

COMPONENTS

Somos así consists of a comprehensive three-level Spanish language program. Components of this second-level textbook, *Somos así 2*, include the following:

- Textbook
- Teacher's Edition
- Workbook
- Workbook Teacher's Edition
- Testing Program (includes Test Booklet, Test Booklet Teacher's Edition and Listening Comprehension Audiocassettes)
- Oral Proficiency Evaluation Manual
- Video Program (includes manual)
- Audiocassette Program (includes manual)

- Computer Software (includes program guide)

- Overhead Transparencies

- Teacher's Resource Binder (TRB) (includes additional Listening Comprehension Activities and Written Activities on blackline duplicating masters, Listening Activities Audiocassettes, Additional Activities Teacher's Edition, Workbook Teacher's Edition, Test Booklet Teacher's Edition, Oral Proficiency Evaluation Manual, Video Program Manual and Audiocassette Program Manual)

Textbook

The textbook contains nine chapters (including the introductory chapter entitled *Introducción*), an appendices section, a Spanish-English and English-Spanish glossary and an index. The *Introducción* consists of six brief high-interest mini-lessons *(Lección A* through *Lección F)* that are easy to teach, lively, communicative, proficiency-based and limited in vocabulary and grammatical explanations. In *Somos Así 2,* these lessons review material presented in the first level of the series, *Somos así 1;* no new material is introduced. With these lessons students will begin to remember and use the Spanish they learned the previous year in enjoyable, authentic contexts, while building confidence and positive motivation from the very first days of class. Succeeding chapters *(Capítulo 1* through *Capítulo 8)* are arranged thematically and consist of two numbered lessons followed by a Spanish reading selection *(Lectura)* and a review lesson (designated by the letters A-H).

Vocabulary has been limited and grammatical structures are constantly reintroduced in order to further improve student mastery of the material. New active words and expressions appear in context within numbered lessons only and in various formats: Some words and expressions appear in bold within dialogs and other expository material and students must discern their meaning from the context in which they are used; more difficult vocabulary appears in bold and is glossed for students; some words and expressions appear in illustrations; and yet other active vocabulary terms may appear in the section *A propósito,* which is explained more thoroughly in the following section descriptions. Regardless of where vocabulary occurs, all words and expressions that students must learn are listed for reference at the end of each lesson.

The choice of which words to illustrate, define or leave for students to discern the meaning of is obviously a subjective one. Every attempt has been made to present new vocabulary in the most pedagogically sound and most appropriate manner to encourage students to think in Spanish, but without making the presentation of new material too difficult for students to enjoy. Words that your students are unable to recognize can be found in the vocabulary glossary that appears at the end of the book.

Each chapter of *Somos así 2* opens with two photo-illustrated pages that visually prepare students for the general cultural and communicative content of the corresponding thematic lessons that follow. Functional objectives and communicative skills that reflect the items students will be learning in the chapter are also listed here.

Numbered lessons begin with a contextualized presentation of new and review vocabulary and grammatical structures. These may take the form of a dialog, narrative or other expository material, accompanied by colorful photographs or illustrations depicting everyday life in the Spanish-speaking world. The people in these scenes represent a cross section of age groups, although the emphasis is on young adults. Be sure to encourage students to read for content and not to rely on glossed vocabulary to translate word-for-word. In the Teacher's Edition the blue cassette symbol indicates which of these items have been recorded as part of the Audiocassette Program.

Following the introductory material are explanatory notes, activities and readings that provide the background necessary to enable students to act and react competently using Spanish in real-life situations. These sections interrelate culture, vocabulary and grammar while inducing students to practice and thus internalize new concepts and skills by engaging in activities that are carefully graded from manipulative (focusing on receptive skills) to personalized and communicative (with an emphasis on productive skills). The main textbook sections include the following:

- *¿Qué comprendiste?*—Dialogs and readings in *Somos así 2* are followed by related questions in the section *¿Qué comprendiste?*, which is designed to check student comprehension. The simple questions, completions, matching, true/false and other comprehension-based formats of the *¿Qué comprendiste?* review the vocabulary, grammatical structures and cultural themes of the preceding expository material and serve as an introduction to the thematic content of the lesson. The presentation of *¿Qué comprendiste?* can be varied each time it appears by trying some of the following: assign items for individual writing practice; have students ask and answer one another in cooperative pairs; use the section as the basis for a class discussion, asking individuals of your choosing to answer orally during the class period; or do the activity as a group activity, starting with one student who answers a question, reads the next question aloud and then chooses a student to respond.

- *Charlando*—Questions in this section are open-ended and personalized, providing realistic and natural writing and speaking opportunities on a variety of everyday topics. Questions in the *Charlando* require thoughtful responses that employ a general understanding of the content of the previous dialog, reading, realia selection, and so on, as well as a specific understanding of Spanish vocabulary, culture and grammar. Students are encouraged to apply what they have just learned while simultaneously drawing upon their own experiences to analyze situations and offer personal opinions about the content. The section is intended to help students internalize new vocabulary and structures while concentrating on the communicative aspect of offering opinions and solving problems in Spanish.

- *A propósito*—Cultural and linguistic notes are presented in the *A propósito* and expand on material presented in other sections of each lesson. These commentaries are intended to heighten the students' appreciation of the target-language culture and to provide insight into daily aspects of Hispanic life. Additional ideas for expanding upon the core content may be suggested in accompanying annotations. The section often presents the opportunity for creative out-of-class projects. Topics covered in the *A propósito* include history, geography, paralinguistic behavioral cues, the arts, cultural and linguistic details from different countries and additional vocabulary in keeping with the authors' goals of providing relevant information that students will find both appealing and useful.

- *Estructura*—These sections summarize the main grammatical points of *Somos así 2*. The clear and concise explanations (often with the addition of colorful charts for easy reference) are followed by activities that practice key grammatical structures and vocabulary in a functional context. These activities have been developed to allow for maximum flexibility since they may be done orally or in writing. For easy identification, activities with answers that have been recorded on audiocassette are indicated in the Teacher's Edition by a blue cassette symbol.

- *Repaso rápido*—Students will already be familiar with the grammatical structures presented in this section, which is meant to be used as a quick review. Exercises follow the *Repaso rápido* to provide additional reinforcement.

- *La práctica hace al maestro*—The section ¡La práctica hace al maestro! (Practice makes perfect!) combines both speaking and writing skills and provides students with personalized opportunities to develop these abilities using the functions, grammar, vocabulary and cultural content of the preceding lesson. Many of the activities involve cooperative learning in which students must work in pairs or small groups in order to accomplish a task. The *A escribir* activity provides developmental practice in creative writing.

Consider using some of the activities from *¡La práctica hace al maestro!* as a quiz or for prescriptive testing in order to determine deficiencies in student understanding of the lesson content, thus allowing time for remediation before end-of-lesson testing. The section also may be used in place of some sections of, or along with, the Testing Program for end-of-lesson summative testing.

- *Vocabulario*—Active vocabulary is introduced in context throughout the lesson in various formats, such as illustrations, dialogs, readings, collages, and so forth, and is listed for reference at the end of every lesson. The list of active vocabulary includes only the words that students must be able to speak, read, write and understand. Words from the list will be included in other components in this Spanish program (i.e., workbook, testing, computer software, videos, etc.).

The *Vocabulario* section indicates new active vocabulary for each lesson. Students may review the list, quizzing themselves to see how many words and expressions they recall. The list also helps teachers hold students accountable for their own learning. English translations are not given here since the list is for reference only. English equivalents may be found in the vocabulary glossary.

- *Lectura*—The *Lectura* provides a formal opportunity for students to improve their ability to read in Spanish. Note for students that it is not essential to understand every word in order to read in Spanish. Equivalents for most unknown words have been provided to help students enjoy the content of the readings without having to look up important but passive vocabulary. All highlighted vocabulary is intended to expand student receptive skills and is not intended for active use at this point.

The presentation of the *Lectura* section is similar to that of the dialogs. There are a variety of possible techniques. You should choose the one that is the most effective for you. It is a good idea to prepare students for the particular content of a reading by asking some general questions on the reading topic, such as the questions found in the *Preparación*. Next, play the first paragraph of the recording of the *Lectura*, using the corresponding audiocassette from the Audiocassette Program. As an alternative, you may choose to read the first paragraph yourself. Read the paragraph again with students following along in the book. Give students a moment to look over the paragraph silently on their own and ask questions. Ask for a student to volunteer to read the paragraph aloud. Continue in this way for subsequent paragraphs.

- *Repaso* (after each even-numbered lesson)—The chapter-ending *Repaso* consists of activities that provide additional written and oral practice on lesson vocabulary, grammatical structures, functions and cultural information. Continuous review helps guarantee retention, reinforcement and mastery of concepts. Review activities further stress the communication aspect of language and are an important part of a proficiency-based curriculum. For example, the sections *Expresiones comunes* and *A crear* suggest activities in which students test themselves on the topics they have studied and apply the vocabulary they have learned to their own lives. Here, too, students are encouraged to broaden their knowledge and hone their communication skills by learning additional thematic vocabulary and by relying on Spanish to convey their thoughts and beliefs. You may choose to use some of the suggested activities for self-testing in preparation for more extensive oral proficiency testing.

Teacher's Edition

The Teacher's Edition offers an in-depth and complete guide to using *Somos así 2* and the accompanying ancillaries, including the following:

- **Front Section**—The front section of this Teacher's Edition contains a scope and sequence chart that lists the functions, grammar, cultural notes and readings found in each chapter; a description of all components for *Somos así 2*; an introductory explanation of the methodology and goals of the textbook; a sample step-by-step approach model lesson plan for teaching *Capítulo 3*, along with methodological suggestions; instructional and functional objectives for each lesson; a list of the content included in each of the eight *Repasos* (review lessons); a comprehensive section offering suggestions for additional activities and games; and a list of useful classroom expressions.

- **Within the Body of the Pupil's Edition**—The Teacher's Edition also contains an annotated version of the student textbook that provides answers to close-ended activities, additional teaching suggestions and cultural notes. These helpful notes and suggestions are located in the margins and within the body of the student textbook.

A blue cassette symbol appears in the Teacher's Edition to indicate the sections of the student textbook that have been recorded and that are part of the *Somos así 2* Audiocassette Program. Although the text for many of these activities is contained in the textbook itself, a separate manual that accompanies the Audiocassette Program provides an exact transcript of the recordings, many of which have been modified so they are more appropriate for speaking and listening practice.

Furthermore, all additional writing and listening activities in the Workbook and Teacher's Resource Binder (referred to here as the TRB) are cross-referenced in the textbook. The following abbreviations in the margins of the Teacher's Edition denote a possible point where these activities might be assigned to students: Workbook activity = WB, TRB writing activity = WA, TRB listening activity = LA. For example, the reference "WB1" that appears on page 2 of *Lección A* indicates that Workbook activity 1 is related to the dialog and illustration on that page of the textbook.

Workbook

The Workbook provides reinforcement and expansion of the functions, grammar, readings and cultural points presented in the textbook. Basic skills are augmented through interesting written activities that emphasize both communication and structural production. The Workbook includes a variety of practice in several different formats to maintain student interest. The level of difficulty of the activities ranges from rote practice of vocabulary and basic activities emphasizing receptive skills in reading to more challenging, open-ended items that emphasize productive skills in writing.

The Workbook presents students with an assortment of activities: reading passages taken from actual newspaper and magazine articles with follow-up questions and exercises; sentence completion; guided compositions; matching activities; practice in geography in mapping activities; word searches; crossword puzzles; and more. Reading, writing, grammar, vocabulary and culture are all given thorough attention in the Workbook.

Workbook Teacher's Edition

The Teacher's Edition of the Workbook includes an overprint that provides answers to close-ended activities in the Workbook.

Testing Program

A proficiency-based curriculum requires a way of testing an individual's attainment of stated objectives. The *Somos así 2* student Testing Program offers comprehensive means for evaluating student performance. The basic program consists of the following components:

- **Test Booklet**—The Test Booklet contains tests for each of the lessons, including the lessons of the *Introducción*. In addition there are comprehensive mid-year and year-end tests. Student answer sheets for listening comprehension tests and for written tests are included in the Test Booklet.

- **Test Booklet Teacher's Edition**—The Test Booklet Teacher's Edition includes the text of the material recorded on audiocassettes for the listening comprehension tests, along with an answer key to these tests. It also includes an answer key for the written tests.

- **Listening Comprehension Audiocassettes**—The *Somos así 2* Testing Program also contains listening comprehension tests. The material for testing listening skills is included on audiocassettes. Student answer sheets are provided in the Test Booklet.

Oral Proficiency Evaluation Manual

The Testing Program can be expanded by evaluating student oral proficiency using the activities included in the Oral Proficiency Evaluation Manual. This component consists of three parts or types of activities: communicative interaction between teacher and student, paired activities that call for student-to-student interaction and illustrations with related questions that students must answer orally in Spanish.

Video Program

The Video Program for *Somos así 2* was filmed on-location in various parts of the Spanish-speaking world using professional actors. The nine episodes, which vary in length from five to eight minutes for each chapter (including the introductory lessons), consist of a continuous storyline that is carefully coordinated to the content of the textbook. The videos depict native speakers in authentic situations employing the communicative functions, structures and vocabulary of *Somos así 2,* thus allowing students an opportunity to see and hear Spanish used in a carefully controlled but realistic and enjoyable context. Some additional words and expressions that are used can be easily understood by the context (motion, action, gestures, background) of the material presented. An accompanying Video Program Manual contains a transcript of the videos, notes about using the program and numerous activities on blackline duplicating masters.

Audiocassette Program

The Audiocassette Program is an integral part of *Somos así 2* since it exposes students to a variety of native speakers' voices with different accents, pronunciation and intonation. The following material has been recorded on audiocassettes and is indicated in this Teacher's Edition of the book by a blue cassette symbol: dialogs, readings and other expository material for listening practice and for dictation; *¿Qué comprendiste?* questions and answers; *Charlando questions;* selected activities related to the *Estructura* and the *Repaso;* and questions and answers in the end-of-chapter section entitled *Lectura.* For additional listening practice, each chapter concludes with a spontaneously recorded dialog or narrative.

Computer Software

The *Somos así 2* Computer Software is coordinated with the content of the textbook. These nine computer diskettes (there is one diskette for the six lessons of the *Introducción* and one for each of the eight chapters) augment, enhance and expand upon the material presented in the textbook and other ancillaries. Each diskette includes grammar explanations, vocabulary-building activities, cloze-readings (students provide missing words from a list to complete the reading), simulation dialogs (students carry on a conversation with the computer) and cultural-enrichment activities in a variety of different formats. Questions for activities are randomly generated so a different sequence as well as some new sentences will appear the next time a student does the same section. A print option allows you to create a hard copy of activity questions for alternative computer-generated testing.

The Computer Software is an excellent device to give students additional practice on lesson content. The diskettes also serve as a useful means of motivating students and expanding upon the core content of *Somos así* for students who require increased individualization or for students who wish to pursue independent study.

The nine diskettes are available for personal computers. An accompanying program guide provides additional details on effective use of this ancillary.

Overhead Transparencies

A set of sixty-four full-color overhead transparencies accompany *Somos así 2*. They offer the basis for a variety of different types of activities including rote review of discreet vocabulary and grammar, mapping activities of the countries students are studying and comprehensive scenes that encourage creative self-expression. Use the transparencies to review and expand the cultural content, grammar, vocabulary and functions that are presented in the textbook and to encourage students to apply their knowledge of Spanish and the Spanish-speaking world.

Teacher's Resource Binder

The Teacher's Resource Binder (TRB) is a handy and practical tool that organizes supplemental teaching materials. Items contained in the TRB include the following:

- **Listening Activities (on blackline duplicating masters)**—These activities consist of listening comprehension practice and are intended to offer students an opportunity to practice their understanding of the content of the corresponding textbook lessons. They are to be used with the Listening Comprehension Audiocassettes, which have been recorded by native speakers and which can be found in a vinyl insert in the Teacher's Resource Binder.

- **Written Activities (on blackline duplicating masters)**—These activities have been provided to increase the convenience and flexibility of teaching with *Somos así 2*. The coordinated activities are sequenced with the content of the textbook and include both reading and writing practice that you may choose to use for enrichment or as a text-related reinforcement of the content of the textbook.

- **Listening Activities Audiocassettes**—These audiocassettes are contained in a vinyl insert in the Teacher's Resource Binder. They offer the recorded version of the Listening Activities.

- **Additional Activities Teacher's Edition**—This booklet contains the answers to the additional Listening Comprehension Activities and Written Activities as well as a transcript of the recorded version of the Listening Activities.

- **Workbook Teacher's Edition**—The Workbook Teacher's Edition provides an overprint of the answers for the Workbook activities.

- **Test Booklet Teacher's Edition**—The Test Booklet Teacher's Edition contains the answers to listening and written tests as well as a transcript of the listening comprehension tests included on audiocassettes in the Testing Program.

- **Oral Proficiency Evaluation Manual**—The materials for the evaluation of oral proficiency consist of three types of activities: communicative interaction between teacher and student, paired activities calling for student-to-student interaction and illustrations with related questions that students must answer orally in Spanish.

- **Video Program Manual**—The Video Program Manual includes a script of the videos provided with *Somos así 2* along with suggestions for incorporating video into the classroom instructional program, previewing and post-viewing activities, comprehension activities and personalized, open-ended activities.

- **Audiocassette Program Manual**—The Audiocassette Program Manual provides a script of the audiocassette material along with the questions and answers included after the expository material for each lesson.

METHODOLOGY

Somos así 2 is a result of an effort to meet the ever-growing need for a foreign language educational program that can be applied in a variety of situations. Using this proficiency-based approach, a positive learning spiral is generated: activities are structured to allow students to apply immediately what they have learned. The resulting feeling of accomplishment leads them back into the textbook where they acquire more skills and information and are then able to draw upon their own personal experience to communicate information, attitudes and opinions in authentic Spanish. The supplemental materials have been designed to support this proficiency-based program. The following are some guidelines to maximize use of the *Somos así 2* curriculum:

Recognition vs. Production—Students are able to recognize new vocabulary and structures before being able to produce them. Errors may occur naturally during the move from recognition to production, but this is an acceptable part of the language-learning process. *Somos así 2* presents new material and then recycles it in a number of different ways in each of the components of the program, thus aiding this process. Some activities dealing with *Estructura*, for example, will promote recognition more than production (especially in the activities immediately after concept presentation). Students will feel more comfortable at the productive levels of communication as they continue in the program and use materials that practice previously learned material. Augmenting the textbook with the Audiocassette Program, Video Program, Computer Software, Workbook, Teacher's Resource Binder and other supplemental materials will prove helpful in developing the ability to produce Spanish in communicative contexts. In particular, activities in the section *¡La práctica hace al maestro!* and the activities in each *Repaso* are intended to stimulate additional production on a communicative level; students may be encouraged further toward production of the target language if they are afforded extra time to prepare these activities. As a general homework assignment, have students scan each lesson for new vocabulary, grammar and the cultural theme. This will speed up recognition and, hence, production.

Pair Work, Group Work and Cooperative Learning—An aim of *Somos así 2* is to allow students ample opportunities for creative self-expression. An additional aim of the program is to broaden that horizon, in particular to take the language-learning process out of the classroom context and into the world. One way to do that is to decrease textbook dependency and to remove the idea that Spanish is a language that exists only in a static environment. The abundant illustrations and photographs in *Somos así 2* reveal Spanish in real-life situations. Each *Capítulo* is organized around a theme that students may apply to their own lives.

Pair work is valuable to encourage the internalization of the target language since it provides students with an authentic communicative setting with real communicative goals. Numerous activities in every lesson are structured for role playing or for open-ended practice in pairs. Group work is also valuable and is most efficient in groups of no more than five members.

To many, cooperative learning involves merely having students work in pairs or small groups practicing material that has been presented in class. This procedure is certainly one aspect of cooperative learning and it is extensively utilized in *Somos así 2.* However, cooperative learning at a more significant level requires that one student relate or share information with another student (or with a small group or even the entire class) that the student has acquired through personal experience or from recent study. Numerous activities in the textbook, in the Teacher's Edition annotations and in the Teacher's Edition introduction address this issue and provide teachers with extensive opportunities to include this type of practice as a normal part of the curriculum.

Activities that students themselves engage in, either in pairs or in small groups, encourage proficiency in a number of ways: More students can use the target language for a more extended period of time than is possible in a teacher-centered activity; students have a feeling of accomplishment in this atmosphere since they are interacting successfully; the teacher is able to meet the needs of more students by circulating among students and correcting or directing where necessary; and most importantly, learning with one's peers results in a nonthreatening learning atmosphere, since the object is communication and not mere correction of errors.

Critical Listening—Perhaps the most basic of all language-learning skills is listening, first for recognition of sounds that convey meaning and later for error correction in pronunciation, structure and so on. Students can develop this skill by listening to the teacher, to the *Somos así* audio components, to themselves and to each other. (At this level, students are able to use critical listening such as identification of structures and self-correction.)

Critical Thinking—It is essential to place emphasis on developing critical thinking skills, or higher order thinking skills, in our students if they are to succeed in school and later in life. An abundance of activities in *Somos así 2* practice critical thinking, in particular in this introduction to the Teacher's Edition under the heading Additional Activities. The cognitive abilities and their associated critical thinking skills included in the program are: knowledge acquisition (locate, define, describe, identify, list, match, name, recite, recall); comprehension (explain, summarize, rewrite, convert, translate, rearrange, paraphrase); analysis (compare and contrast, interpret, outline, subdivide, order, categorize, distinguish); evaluation (criticize, conclude, support, justify); synthesis (associate, combine, compile, rearrange, plan, generalize); and application (compose, create, design, produce).

Language Through Action—While many educators recognize the importance of the senses (sight, hearing, and so forth) in the language-learning process, the use of physical action and reaction to verbal stimuli as an asset to language acquisition has not been thoroughly exploited. One excellent technique used in second-language learning is Total Physical Response (TPR). Since TPR involves a student's physical memory, it is an aid in internalizing new concepts or vocabulary and in recycling those already learned. One TPR activity might require you to give a series of commands to students, which you would adjust according to the ability of the class. You can contextualize the vocabulary and structures based upon the material you wish to present for that class session.

Many teachers of foreign languages have experimented with TPR but often find it burdensome to incorporate in their lessons on a regular basis because it generally requires an extra effort on their part to prepare materials pertinent to the lesson at hand. Furthermore, some teachers are unaware of methods for progressing from mere physical responses on the part of the students to verbal responses. Likewise, the integration of command forms with the present, past, future, and so forth can be puzzling and complex. To address this issue, complete and clear instructions and guidelines are included with the TPR activities in *Somos así 2*.

These are but a few of the language-teaching approaches and methods incorporated into *Somos así 2*. A glance at the textbook, Teacher's Edition and the wide array of ancillaries for each level of the program will indicate that every effort has been made to assure the teacher a most complete and effective program of instruction based on up-to-date language-teaching approaches and methods.

Note: In *Somos así 2*, instructions for activities are given in the *tú* form. By requiring that students use the *Ud.* form of verbs with you and by suggesting that they learn to recognize and use the *tú* form of verbs with their peers, you will increase students' exposure to both forms. *Vosotros* has been introduced as a word, but students are not required to use the *vosotros* form of verbs. If you decide to teach using *vosotros*, modify activities to include practice of both the *Uds.* and the *vosotros* forms.

TEACHING SUGGESTIONS

Model Chapter *(Capítulo 3)*

This section of the introduction is intended to show how you might structure lesson plans for *Somos así 2*, allowing approximately four weeks to complete *Lecciones A-F* of the *Introducción* and four weeks per *Capítulo* (about ten class sessions per numbered *Lección*). Because instructional objectives and the length of classes vary greatly, and since ability levels among students are usually considerably different within one class, it would be impossible to provide a detailed lesson plan that would suit every teacher's needs and that would apply to all students using this Spanish language instructional program. In addition, some teachers may not have available to them all the components that make up the program. Consequently, the model lesson plan is intended as a sample and should be modified according to your own teaching situation.

An effort has been made in *Somos así 2* to combine a variety of different kinds of activities along with cultural information that will appeal to students with different learning styles, interests and needs. Some activities practice simple tasks, such as vocabulary enhancement, while others provide more challenging contextualized practice of skills. This combination is intended to help students develop their ability to use Spanish in a logical step-by-step fashion, with the ultimate goal of helping students learn to communicate in authentic Spanish. Since many of the activities require students to work in pairs or small groups, the traditional teacher-centered class will seem more student-centered and provide additional opportunities for students to actually use the language more during class time. The teacher's role, however, remains of utmost importance. Be certain to circulate among students to ensure that they remain on task and to provide assistance as needed.

Somos así 2 offers the flexibility of covering material in the textbook and ancillaries to suit individual needs. You may omit some activities and cover the various sections of a lesson with the degree of thoroughness suggested by student needs, time and your own personal teaching style or school resources. In general, try to vary your presentations by using as many different resources as possible in order to recombine similar material for your students' diverse learning styles. For example, the Audiocassette Program and the Teacher's Resource Binder offer listening comprehension practice; the Video Program allows students an opportunity to observe native speakers using Spanish in contexts that require skills your students are learning;

the Computer Software tutorials and games individualize and personalize instruction; Overhead Transparencies offer visual support of spoken Spanish and can serve to practice both rote material as well as to provide situational contexts for conversations; the textbook, Workbook and TRB activities offer additional writing practice.

Capítulo 3 (Lecciones 5, 6 and *Repaso C)* has been selected as the model chapter, since it contains all elements of a typical chapter. Activities are based upon a daily, fifty-minute class period. Some activities and *A propósito* cultural notes may be omitted, depending upon the needs and time limitations set by individual circumstances. The reading section entitled *Lectura* and *Repaso* activities are optional, thus offering you additional flexibility in matching content to the needs, interests and curriculum requirements of your own particular situation.

Dialogs, other narrative material and many activities in *Somos así 2* have been recorded and thus offer you additional choices in presenting or reviewing the chapter content. For example, you may choose to have students listen to a recorded activity before going to the textbook, or you may choose instead to use the audiocassette as additional reinforcement after having completed the activity in the textbook. Recorded activities are indicated by a blue cassette symbol in the margins of the Teacher's Edition of the textbook.

In addition, the many ancillaries already discussed in this front section are available to supplement the textbook. These numerous program components provide an abundance of textbook-related activities to provide teaching formats that will enable you to customize your teaching to the many and varied learning styles and needs of your students.

Since every teacher has his or her own approach to the subject of homework, and due to the extensive variety offered by the *Somos así 2* support materials, specific homework assignments in this model are limited to activities that appear in the textbook. However, suggestions for including activities from the accompanying ancillaries have been offered to give you an idea as to some possible variations the teaching program offers. You should try to include an assortment of different activities, choosing some from the textbook and others from the ancillaries (such as the Workbook, the Teacher's Edition, etc.).

Day 1

1. Return tests *(Capítulo 2, Lección 4)* and go over questions or problems, as necessary.

2. If you have not done so during the previous class session, present the functions and objectives for *Capítulo 3* (p. 173) and for *Lección 5.* (See

the section entitled Instructional Objectives in this front section of *Somos así 2*. Be sure to stress the communicative functions that can be found in the blue annotations on the first page of *Lección 5*.)

3. Warm-up: In order to bridge from one lesson to the next, review previously learned content and expressions that will help the class understand the dialog entitled *En el parque de atracciones* (p. 174): *¿Te gustan los parques de atracciones? ¿Vas con tu familia o con tus amigos? ¿Cuál es tu actividad favorita en los parques? ¿Cómo se llama tu parque favorito?* Have students look at the illustration (ask them to cover up or ignore the written Spanish for the moment). Then ask students to imagine who the people are, where they are, what they are doing, and so forth.

4. Show the class where El Salvador is located using the maps in the front of the book or the transparencies that are part of this program.

5. Present the lesson-opening dialog for *Lección 5, En el parque de atracciones* (p. 174). Have students listen to the recording of the dialog, noting that they are not expected to understand everything they hear. (The blue cassette symbol in the margins of the Teacher's Edition indicates that this activity has been recorded and can be found on the corresponding audiocassette from the Audiocassette Program for *Somos así 2*.) Encourage students to listen carefully to the sounds, tone and rhythm of the language, while trying to make educated guesses about the meaning of new words and expressions. Have students learn to look at illustrations, photographs and contextual clues to determine meaning. Spanish and English equivalents are provided following narratives for some difficult-to-understand active vocabulary. New grammar will be explained later in the lesson. Words that your students are unable to recognize can be found in the vocabulary glossary that appears at the end of the book. If you choose to have students open their books and look at the illustration as they listen, ask them to cover the written dialog for the present so they can practice and improve the important skill of listening to spoken Spanish without written support.

6. Play the recorded dialog again as students follow along silently. Ask simple questions (*¿Cuántas personas hay en el diálogo? ¿Dónde están? ¿Cómo se llaman? ¿De qué hablan?*), then have students practice the dialog together in pairs as you move around the classroom checking for correct pronunciation. Activity 1 of *Lección 5* in the *Somos así 2* Workbook (coded in blue in the teacher's annotations as WB1) and activity 1 of the *Lección 5* TRB written activities (coded in blue in the teacher's annotations as WA1) offer additional practice and reinforce the content of pages 174-175. Furthermore, the section of this Teacher's Edition entitled Additional Activities offers supplementary activities for pages 174-175 that you may choose to do with your class.

7. Do the *¿Qué comprendiste?* (p. 175). You can extend the activity by asking the additional questions that appear in blue in the Teacher's Edition (p. 175). On occasion you may decide to paraphrase or modify questions slightly to add variety. For example, the question *¿Quién molestaba a unas chicas?* could be restated as *¿Cómo molestaba el hermano de Rocío a unas chicas?* Discuss the *Charlando* questions that appear on p. 175.

8. Have students do activity 1 (p. 175).

9. If you have the *Somos así 2* Video Program, consider showing the corresponding segment with the sound turned off during the first day of a new *Capítulo,* or at another more appropriate time of your choosing. Have students observe and make cultural comparisons with their own lives. Ask students to draw conclusions about the content, much as they might in doing a pre-reading activity for a Spanish reading or if they were doing a pre-listening activity for a Spanish dialog.

10. If you have the Computer Software, allow students to use the programs for individualizing learning any day during the course of teaching a *Capítulo* for reinforcing previously taught content or for broadening the presentation of new material where it is justified.

11. Before assigning homework each day, summarize the main points of the day's lesson to give adequate closure.

Assignment:

1. Have students read the *A propósito* entitled *El Salvador* (p. 176).

2. Assign activity 2 (p. 177) or any activities from the *Somos así 2* ancillaries that you deem appropriate. You may wish to give students several days to complete the publicity posters on El Salvador.

Day 2

1. Warm-up: Using the overhead transparency map of Central America or the map at the front of the book, discuss El Salvador. Note points of interest and talk about the information provided in the *A propósito* (p. 176). Then ask students questions as part of an ongoing assessment of their proficiency in using Spanish and their knowledge of the culture of the Spanish-speaking world.

2. Have students practice the dialog *En el parque de atracciones* (p. 174). Ask for volunteers to read aloud and work on pronunciation. Have students form pairs to play the parts of Rocío and Juan.

3. Have students read aloud the three paragraphs of the *A propósito* on El Salvador. Activity 2 for *Lección 5* of the TRB listening activities (coded in blue in the teacher's annotations as *LA 2*) offers additional practice

over the content of this *A propósito*. Workbook activity 2 for *Lección 5* (coded in blue in the teacher's annotations as *WB2*) also pertains to this *A propósito*.

4. Introduce the *Estructura* on *El imperfecto de los verbos regulares* (pp. 177-178). Return to the dialog *En el parque de atracciones* (p. 174) and ask students to find examples of the imperfect tense *(había, comía, gritaban, pasaba, molestaba, miraban)*. Do activity 3 (p. 179) orally. Activity 1 of the textbook section entitled *Repaso C* (p. 220) offers an activity to practice and reinforce the imperfect tense. (*Repaso* activities should be assigned to individuals, to groups or to the entire class at your discretion.) The margins of the Teacher's Edition contain blue annotations that indicate corresponding *Repaso* activities (in this case, for example, *R1*).

5. Extend the introduction of the imperfect tense by presenting the *A propósito* entitled *Los usos del imperfecto* (p. 180). Then do activity 5 (p. 181).

6. Before assigning homework, summarize the main points of the day's lesson to give adequate closure.

Assignment:

1. Have students do activity 4 (p. 179) and activity 6 (p. 181).

2. Assign activities from the *Repaso C* or *Somos así 2* ancillaries that you deem appropriate.

Day 3

1. Warm-up: Review the formation and use of the imperfect tense. Do a rapid-paced drill of common *-ar, -er,* and *-ir* verbs asking for the correct verb ending as you cue students with different subjects.

2. Practice verbs that students have seen by asking for choral response of the *yo* form of the imperfect tense. (Prompt students with several of the verbs.) Then ask for the *tú* form and prompt students with several verbs. Continue in this way until you complete all the subject pronouns. Then ask simple, personalized questions in the imperfect.

3. Review activity 4 (p. 179) and activity 6 (p. 181).

4. As time allows, you may wish to do some of the supplementary activities indicated in blue in the margin of the Teacher's Edition. These include Workbook activities 5 and 6, writing activity 2 (included in the TRB) and activities 3 and 4 of the *Repaso*.

5. Preview the dialog *En el jardín zoológico* (p. 182) by asking students to say what they know about the conversation based upon the title and what they see in the illustration. Play the recorded dialog as students

follow along silently. Ask simple questions to guide students. Have students practice the dialog, repeating after the native speakers when there are pauses on the audiocassette. Ask for volunteers to read the two dialog parts aloud.

6. Do the *A propósito* on *¿Qué es América?* and cover the *¿Qué comprendiste?* section (p. 183). Note the additional questions in the margin of the Teacher's Edition.

7. Do the *¿Qué comprendiste?* (p. 183).

8. Discuss the *A propósito* entitled *¿Los nombres de animales o de personas?* (p. 183). End the class with a thoughtful discussion of cultural pluralism, basing your discussion upon the teacher's annotation entitled *Creatividad mental* (p. 183).

9. Before assigning homework, summarize the main points of the day's lesson to give adequate closure.

Assignment:

1. Have students prepare answers to the *Charlando* questions (p. 184).

2. Assign activities from the *Repaso C* or *Somos así 2* ancillaries that you deem appropriate.

Day 4

1. Warm-up: Have some students present their publicity posters on El Salvador.

2. Review the questions in the *Charlando* (p. 184), asking any additional questions from the blue annotations that appear in the Teacher's Edition, as time allows.

3. Present the *Estructura* on the imperfect of *ser, ir* and *ver* (p. 184).

4. Discuss additional uses for the imperfect tense that are presented in the *A propósito* entitled *Los usos del imperfecto: un poco más* (p. 185).

5. Do activity 7 (p. 186).

6. Consider doing some of the additional activities noted in the margin of the Teacher's Edition: Workbook activity 9, writing activity 5 or listening activity 5 from the TRB or *Repaso* activity 6.

7. Before assigning homework, summarize the main points of the day's lesson to give adequate closure. Consider giving a quiz over the imperfect tense, over vocabulary or over some topic or discreet point from the lesson tomorrow.

Assignment:

1. Have students do activity 8 (p. 187) and activity 9 (p. 188).

2. Assign activities from the *Repaso C* or *Somos así 2* ancillaries that you deem appropriate.

3. Inform students whether you will be giving a quiz tomorrow.

Day 5

1. Warm-up: Briefly review the vocabulary from this lesson. Try the following activity to review material while you take attendance: Have students prepare one question or statement from the lesson; as you call roll, students respond with the question or statement rather than *aquí* or *presente*. For this lesson, have students state what they were doing before class began (using the imperfect tense).

2. Review the formation of the imperfect tense, discussing any difficulties students may be having.

3. Review activity 8 (p. 187) and activity 9 (p. 188).

4. Do activity 10 (p. 188) as a class writing answers on the chalkboard.

5. You may wish to give a quiz over a discreet item such as a grammar point from the lesson, such as the imperfect tense of *ser, ir* and *ver* or the items covered in the *A propósito* (p. 185). As another option, consider using any free time to ask students questions about what they were doing yesterday before they went to dinner in order to check pronunciation or to evaluate student oral proficiency using Spanish. (Doing these activities on an ongoing basis will allow you to more thoroughly and more fairly evaluate student performance while simultaneously helping students prepare for the lesson-ending testing and oral proficiency evaluation.)

6. Before assigning homework, summarize the main points of the day's lesson to give adequate closure.

Assignment:

1. Assign activities from the *Repaso C* or *Somos así 2* ancillaries that you deem appropriate.

Day 6

1. Warm-up: If you gave a quiz during the previous class session, review the results with students.

2. Go over any activities you assigned from *Repaso C* or the additional activities in the ancillaries.

3. Present the *A propósito* (p. 189). Note that Workbook activity 12 pertains to this section.

4. Do activity 11 (p. 189) orally or in writing.

5. Have students work in pairs on activity 12 (p. 189). Note the additional activity suggested in the margin.

6. Present information in the *A propósito* (p. 190), noting especially spelling, accent marks and the dieresis on *nicaragüense*. See the notes and the activities from the ancillaries as indicated in the margins of the Teacher's Edition.

7. Have students work in groups of three on activity 13 (p. 191).

8. Before assigning homework, summarize the main points of the day's lesson to give adequate closure.

Assignment:

1. Have students prepare questions and answers for activity 14 (p. 191).

2. Assign activities from the *Repaso C* or *Somos así 2* ancillaries that you deem appropriate.

Day 7

1. Warm-up: Discuss any problems students had with activity 14 (p. 191).

2. Have students work in pairs on activity 14 (p. 191).

3. Present the *Repaso rápido* on *ser* versus *estar* (p. 192).

4. Do activity 15 (p. 193).

5. Have students form pairs to do activity A of the section *¡La práctica hace al maestro!* (p. 194).

6. Before assigning homework, summarize the main points of the day's lesson to give adequate closure.

Assignment:

1. Have students do activity 16 (p. 193).

2. Assign activities from the *Repaso C* or *Somos así 2* ancillaries that you deem appropriate.

Day 8

1. Warm-up: Be sure to practice the vocabulary (p. 195) with students on an ongoing basis by trying the following: First, model the pronunciation of several words and phrases from the vocabulary list for student repetition; select several words and phrases for individual students to use orally in sentences.

2. Discuss any difficulties students may have had with activity 16 (p. 193). Follow up the discussion by playing the audiocassette of activity 16.

3. If you have the Computer Software, use the programs for individualizing learning, for reinforcing previously taught content or for broadening the presentation of new material where it is justified.

4. Before assigning homework, summarize the main points of the day's lesson to give adequate closure.

Assignment:

1. Inform students about tomorrow's test on listening comprehension and/or oral proficiency. (Determine if or how you will evaluate oral proficiency by reading the introductory matter to the *Somos así 2* Oral Proficiency Evaluation Manual.)

2. Have students prepare the composition for activity B of the section *¡La práctica hace al maestro!* (p. 194). Inform students if (or when) you expect the compositions to be turned in and how they will be used (as a quiz, as a class review, and so forth).

3. Assign activities from the *Repaso C* or *Somos así 2* ancillaries that you deem appropriate.

Day 9

1. Review the compositions students wrote, examining problems and assisting with difficulties. Whether you are going to collect the compositions for a grade or not, you may choose to allow students an extra day to make corrections based upon this classroom discussion.

2. If you are going to split the exam for *Lección 5* in two, administer the listening comprehension test today. This spoken portion is contained on the audiocassettes that are part of the Testing Program. A written audiocassette script with all exam questions and an answer key are also available. (You can use all or part of the Oral Proficiency Evaluation Manual activities if you have chosen to test for oral proficiency at this time.)

3. If you have the Computer Software, this would be a good time to allow students access to the diskette for this lesson for review or enrichment or to offer capable students the opportunity to move ahead at their own pace.

4. Summarize the material that will be tested during the next class session. This will allow students the opportunity to ask you for help with specific problems they have encountered over the last nine days.

Assignment:

1. Prepare for the (written) test on *Lección 5.*

Day 10

1. If you are going to collect student compositions for activity B of the section *¡La práctica hace al maestro!* (p. 194), consider doing so now.

2. Test students on *Lección 5* using the Testing Program that accompanies *Somos así 2.* (If you already have administered the listening portion of the test and if you have concluded any oral proficiency evaluation you intended to complete, have students complete the written portion for *Lección 5* of the Testing Program.)

3. If time allows, consider previewing the next lesson by presenting the functions and objectives for *Lección 6.* (See the section entitled Instructional Objectives in this introduction to the Teacher's Edition. Be sure to stress the communicative functions that can be found in the blue annotations on the first page of *Lección 6.*)

Day 11

1. Return tests *(Capítulo 3, Lección 5)* and go over questions or problems, as necessary.

2. Present the functions and objectives for *Lección 6.* (See the section entitled Instructional Objectives in this introduction to the Teacher's Edition of *Somos así 2.* Be sure to stress the communicative functions that can be found in the blue annotations on the first page of *Lección 6.*)

3. Warm-up: Give students a brief introduction to Honduras by showing where the country is located, using the maps in the front of the book or the transparencies that are part of this program.

4. Have students look at the illustrations that accompany *En el circo* (p. 196). Ask students to look for cues that will help them discern what the dialog is about.

5. Play the recording of the contents of the dialog (p. 196) as students follow along silently. Ask the *¿Qué comprendiste?* questions (p. 197). Extend the activity by asking the additional questions that appear in blue in the Teacher's Edition (p. 197).

6. Ask the *Charlando* questions (p. 197), including the additional items included in the margin of the Teacher's Edition.

7. Have students work in pairs to practice the dialog on p. 196.

8. Have students work in pairs on activity 1 (p. 197).

9. Before assigning homework, summarize the main points of the day's lesson to give adequate closure.

Assignment:

1. Have students read the *A propósito* entitled *Honduras* (p. 198).

2. Assign activity 2 (p. 199) and any activities from the *Repaso C* or *Somos así 2* ancillaries that you deem appropriate.

Day 12

1. Warm-up: Using the overhead transparency map of Central America, or the map at the front of the book, talk with the class about the *A propósito* on Honduras (p. 198), asking students to identify where some of the places mentioned in the reading are located.

2. Ask for volunteers to read aloud a few sentences each from the reading on Honduras and work on pronunciation.

3. Review the questions and answers for activity 2 (p. 199).

4. Present the *Estructura* (p. 199).

5. Practice the forms of *-ísimo* and then do activity 3 (p. 200). You may wish to use the audio recording that accompanies this activity.

6. Do activity 4 or assign the activity as homework for tomorrow.

7. Before assigning homework, summarize the main points of the day's lesson to give adequate closure.

Assignment:

1. Have students study the *Repaso rápido* and prepare activity 5 (p. 202). Assign activity 4 if you did not cover it in class.

2. Assign activities from the *Repaso C* or *Somos así 2* ancillaries that you deem appropriate.

Day 13

1. Warm-up: Review the homework assignments, examining problems and assisting with difficulties.

2. Go over the *Repaso rápido* and activity 5.

3. Do activity 6 (p. 203).

4. Introduce and practice the *Estructura* on adjectives (p. 203).

5. Allow students a few minutes to prepare activity 7 (p. 205) and then prepare the answers as a group activity in class.

6. Do activity 8 (p. 206).

7. Before assigning homework, summarize the main points of the day's lesson to give adequate closure.

Assignment:

1. Have students do the creative writing practice of activity 9 (p. 206).

2. Assign activities from the *Repaso C* or *Somos así 2* ancillaries that you deem appropriate.

Day 14

1. Collect the maps that students prepared on Central America if you made this assignment (*Repaso* activity 8, p. 222).

2. Warm-up: Review the homework assignments.

3. Have students work in pairs on activity 9 (p. 206), correcting each other's errors. Circulate among students and offer assistance as needed. Then call on several students to read their corrected compositions aloud to the class.

4. Present the *Repaso rápido* (p. 207) and have students work in pairs on activity 10 (p. 207).

5. Have students look at the illustration (p. 208) and preview the dialog *En la finca* (p. 208), going over the vocabulary presented in the artwork.

6. Play the audio recording of *En la finca* (p. 208) and have students read along silently. Then have several students practice dialog aloud in pairs.

7. Do the section *¿Qué comprendiste?* (p. 209). Additional questions appear in blue in the Teacher's Edition (p. 209).

8. Ask the questions in the *Charlando* (p. 209). If time permits, ask some of the additional questions that appear in blue in the Teacher's Edition (p. 209).

9. Before assigning homework, summarize the main points of the day's lesson to give adequate closure.

Assignment:

1. Have students prepare activity 11 (p. 209).

2. Assign activities from the *Repaso C* or *Somos así 2* ancillaries that you deem appropriate.

Day 15

1. Warm-up: Go over activity 11 and any other assignments you may have made. Occasionally, you may wish to follow up an activity imme-

diately using the audiocassette that contains the same activity in order to give students additional oral practice on familiar material. If you choose to try this with activity 11, have students close their books and respond to the aural cues provided on the corresponding audiocassette.

2. Discuss the information provided in the illustration *¿Qué dicen los animales?* and the *A propósito* (p. 210) that follows.

3. Do activity 12 (p. 210).

4. Have students work in pairs on activity 13 (p. 211).

5. Present the *Estructura* on the long forms of the possessive adjectives. Note the blue codes in the margin of the Teacher's Edition, referring to additional activities in the Workbook and TRB.

6. Go over activity 14 (p. 212) and then have students work in pairs to practice the dialog.

7. At this point, you may wish to give a quiz over a discreet item such as vocabulary or a grammar point from the lesson.

8. Before assigning homework, summarize the main points of the day's lesson to give adequate closure.

Assignment:

1. Have students prepare the questions and answers for activity 15 (p. 213).

2. Assign activities from the *Repaso C* or *Somos así 2* ancillaries that you deem appropriate.

Day 16

1. Warm-up: Review activity 15 (p. 213) and any other assignments you may have given.

2. Have students work in pairs on activity 16 (p. 213).

3. Present the *A propósito* (p. 213).

4. Do activity 17 (p. 214). For additional listening practice you may wish to use the audio recording that accompanies this activity.

5. Do activity 18 (p. 214).

6. Go over the *A propósito* (p. 214) and do activity 19 (p. 215). Note that this activity may be done orally or in writing. The recorded version is available on audiocassette.

7. Go over the *A propósito* (p. 215) and do activity 20.

8. Before assigning homework, summarize the main points of the day's lesson to give adequate closure.

Assignment:

1. Assign activity B (p. 216).

2. Assign activities from the *Repaso C* or *Somos así 2* ancillaries that you deem appropriate.

Day 17

1. Warm-up: Review the vocabulary (p. 217) for *Lección 6*.

2. Working in pairs, have students do activity A (p. 216).

3. Have students work in small groups to help each other correct errors in their compositions written for activity B (p. 216). Then have several students read their compositions aloud to the group. Inform students whether you will be collecting their compositions for a grade.

4. Review the comparative and the superlative of adjectives in *Lección C*.

5. Introduce the *Lectura* (p. 218) by asking questions from the section *Preparación* (p. 218).

6. If you have the Computer Software, use the programs for individualizing learning, for reinforcing previously taught content or for broadening the presentation of new material where it is justified.

7. Before assigning homework, summarize the main points of the day's lesson to give adequate closure.

Assignment:

1. Have students read the *Lectura* on the circus (p. 219). Be sure to encourage students to read for ideas rather than look up every word they do not recognize. Have students prepare answers to the questions in the section *¿Qué comprendiste?* (p. 219).

2. Assign activities from the *Repaso C* or *Somos así 2* ancillaries that you deem appropriate.

Day 18

1. Warm-up: Play the recording of the contents of the *Lectura* (p. 219) as students read along silently. Then ask for volunteers to read aloud and work on pronunciation.

2. Review the questions for the *¿Qué comprendiste?* (p. 219). Ask each question two or three times of different students, modifying each question slightly as necessary to maintain attention and add variety. Additional questions appear in blue in the Teacher's Edition of the textbook (p. 219).

3. Discuss the *Charlando* questions (p. 219).

4. If you have the *Somos así 2* Video Program, consider showing the corresponding segment at this point, having students do appropriate follow-up activities.

5. If you have the Computer Software, use the programs for individualizing learning, for reinforcing previously taught content or for broadening the presentation of new material where it is justified.

6. Before assigning homework, summarize the main points of the day's lesson to give adequate closure.

Assignment:

1. Assign activities from the *Repaso C* or *Somos así 2* ancillaries that you deem appropriate.

Day 19

1. Warm-up: Review assignments with students.

2. If you are going to split the exam for *Lección 6* in two, administer the listening comprehension test today. This spoken portion of the exam is contained on the audiocassettes that are part of the Testing Program. A written tape script with all exam questions and an answer key are also available. (You can use all or part of the Oral Proficiency Evaluation Manual activities if you have chosen to test for oral proficiency at this time.)

3. If you already have not introduced the *Somos así 2* video for *Capítulo 3*, consider showing the corresponding segment at this point, having students do appropriate follow-up activities.

4. If you have the Computer Software, this would be a good time to allow students access to the diskette for this lesson for review or enrichment or to offer capable students the opportunity to move ahead at their own pace.

5. Summarize the material that will be tested during the next class session. This will allow students the opportunity to ask you for help with specific problems they have encountered over the last nine days.

Assignment:

1. Prepare for the (written) test on *Lección 6*.

Day 20

1. If you are going to collect student compositions on activity B of the section *¡La práctica hace al maestro!* (p. 216), consider doing so now.

2. Test students on *Lección 6* using the Testing Program that accompanies *Somos así 2*. (If you already have administered the listening portion of

the test and if you have concluded any oral proficiency evaluation you intended to complete, have students complete the written portion for *Lección 6* of the Testing Program.)

3. If time allows, and if you have the *Somos así* Video Program, consider viewing the corresponding segment at this point, having students do appropriate follow-up activities.

4. If time allows, consider previewing the next chapter by presenting the functions and objectives for *Capítulo 4* (p. 226) and for *Lección 7*. (See the section entitled Instructional Objectives in this introduction to the Teacher's Edition of *Somos así 2*. Be sure to stress the communicative functions that can be found in the blue annotations on the first page of *Lección 7*.)

INSTRUCTIONAL OBJECTIVES

Introducción

Lección A

After completing all material in this lesson, students should be able to:

1. seek and provide personal information
2. talk about everyday activities
3. describe the weather
4. indicate a length of time
5. summarize cultural information about Chile
6. respond with actions to commands and verbally to related questions (TPR)
7. engage in open-ended, personalized communication in pairs and small groups (cooperative learning)
8. use critical thinking to perform tasks related to the Spanish language and Hispanic culture

Lección B

After completing all material in this lesson, students should be able to:

1. seek and provide personal information
2. talk about family and friends

3. talk about everyday activities

4. use the numbers 0-999,999

5. talk about dates and special days

6. tell time

7. summarize cultural information about Mexico

8. respond with actions to commands and verbally to related questions (TPR)

9. engage in open-ended, personalized communication in pairs and small groups (cooperative learning)

10. use critical thinking to perform tasks related to the Spanish language and Hispanic culture

Lección C

After completing all material in this lesson, students should be able to:

1. compare quantity, quality, age and size

2. refer to what has just happened

3. talk about the future

4. seek and provide personal information

5. discuss schedules

6. talk about everyday activities

7. respond with actions to commands and verbally to related questions (TPR)

8. engage in open-ended, personalized communication in pairs and small groups (cooperative learning)

9. use critical thinking to perform tasks related to the Spanish language and Hispanic culture

Lección D

After completing all material in this lesson, students should be able to:

1. seek and provide personal information

2. talk about everyday activities

3. discuss schedules

4. state what is happening right now

5. talk about the future

6. respond with actions to commands and verbally to related questions (TPR)

7. engage in open-ended, personalized communication in pairs and small groups (cooperative learning)

8. use critical thinking to perform tasks related to the Spanish language and Hispanic culture

Lección E

After completing all material in this lesson, students should be able to:

1. talk about the past

2. talk about everyday activities

3. talk about family and friends

4. use the numbers 0-999,999

5. tell time

6. discuss schedules

7. seek and provide personal information

8. talk about dates and special days

9. respond with actions to commands and verbally to related questions (TPR)

10. engage in open-ended, personalized communication in pairs and small groups (cooperative learning)

11. use critical thinking to perform tasks related to the Spanish language and Hispanic culture

Lección F

After completing all material in this lesson, students should be able to:

1. seek and provide personal information

2. talk about everyday activities

3. talk about family and friends

4. talk about the future

5. refer to what has just happened

6. discuss schedules

7. state what is happening right now

8. talk about dates and special days

9. talk about the past

10. respond with actions to commands and verbally to related questions (TPR)

11. engage in open-ended, personalized communication in pairs and small groups (cooperative learning)

12. use critical thinking to perform tasks related to the Spanish language and Hispanic culture

Lección 1

After completing all material in this lesson, students should be able to:

1. talk about everyday activities

2. express annoyance

3. seek and provide personal information

4. discuss personal grooming

5. compare and contrast

6. recognize and identify Hispanic influences in the United States

7. state when things are done

8. express past actions and events

9. identify items in the bathroom

10. point something out

11. write about everyday activities

12. respond with actions to commands and verbally to related questions (TPR)

13. engage in open-ended, personalized communication in pairs and small groups (cooperative learning)

14. use critical thinking to perform tasks related to the Spanish language and Hispanic culture

Lección 2

After completing all material in this lesson, students should be able to:

1. seek and provide personal information

2. discuss health

3. give and take instructions

4. recognize and use expressions in a doctor's office

5. talk about everyday activities

6. recognize and identify Hispanic influences in the United States

7. identify parts of the body

8. write about everyday activities

9. respond with actions to commands and verbally to related questions (TPR)

10. engage in open-ended, personalized communication in pairs and small groups (cooperative learning)

11. use critical thinking to perform tasks related to the Spanish language and Hispanic culture

Lección 3

After completing all material in this lesson, students should be able to:

1. ask and give directions

2. identify places in the city

3. discuss what is sold in specific stores

4. tell someone what to do

5. order from a menu in a restaurant

6. advise and suggest

7. summarize cultural information about Mexico

8. talk about the foods of several Spanish-speaking parts of the world

9. respond with actions to commands and verbally to related questions (TPR)

10. engage in open-ended, personalized communication in pairs and small groups (cooperative learning)

11. use critical thinking to perform tasks related to the Spanish language and Hispanic culture

Lección 4

After completing all material in this lesson, students should be able to:

1. ask and give directions

2. identify places in the city

3. tell someone what to do

4. discuss who and what people know

5. talk about everyday activities

6. tell others what not to do

7. advise and suggest

8. identify parts of a car

9. advise others in writing

10. summarize cultural information about Mexico

11. recognize some street signs

12. respond with actions to commands and verbally to related questions (TPR)

13. engage in open-ended, personalized communication in pairs and small groups (cooperative learning)

14. use critical thinking to perform tasks related to the Spanish language and Hispanic culture

Lección 5

After completing all material in this lesson, students should be able to:

1. seek and provide personal information

2. describe in the past

3. talk about activities at a special event

4. identify animals

5. express quantities

6. provide background information about the past

7. indicate past intentions

8. discuss nationality

9. summarize cultural information about El Salvador

10. respond with actions to commands and verbally to related questions (TPR)

11. engage in open-ended, personalized communication in pairs and small groups (cooperative learning)

12. use critical thinking to perform tasks related to the Spanish language and Hispanic culture

Lección 6

After completing all material in this lesson, students should be able to:

1. seek and provide personal information

2. provide background information about the past

3. describe in the past

4. talk about activities at a special event

5. add emphasis to a description

6. recognize and express size

7. state possession

8. identify sounds that animals make

9. summarize information about Honduras

10. respond with actions to commands and verbally to related questions (TPR)

11. engage in open-ended, personalized communication in pairs and small groups (cooperative learning)

12. use critical thinking to perform tasks related to the Spanish language and Hispanic culture

Lección 7

After completing all material in this lesson, students should be able to:

1. talk about what someone remembers

2. seek and provide personal information

3. describe clothing

4. report past actions and events

5. talk about everyday activities

6. identify foods

7. use metric weights and measurements

8. read and order from a menu

9. write about the past

10. summarize cultural information about Cuba

11. respond with actions to commands and verbally to related questions (TPR)

12. engage in open-ended, personalized communication in pairs and small groups (cooperative learning)

13. use critical thinking to perform tasks related to the Spanish language and Hispanic culture

Lección 8

After completing all material in this lesson, students should be able to:

1. express opinions
2. talk about everyday activities
3. ask for advice
4. state what was happening at a specific time
5. describe clothing
6. describe how something was done
7. express length of time
8. discuss food preparation
9. write a description about the past
10. summarize cultural information about the Caribbean
11. respond with actions to commands and verbally to related questions (TPR)
12. engage in open-ended, personalized communication in pairs and small groups (cooperative learning)
13. use critical thinking to perform tasks related to the Spanish language and Hispanic culture

Lección 9

After completing all material in this lesson, students should be able to:

1. tell someone what to do
2. report what others say
3. state wishes and preferences
4. talk about everyday activities
5. talk about family
6. make a request
7. advise and suggest
8. summarize cultural information on Bolivia
9. describe specific architectural treatments for houses in Spanish-speaking parts of the world
10. respond with actions to commands and verbally to related questions (TPR)

11. engage in open-ended, personalized communication in pairs and small groups (cooperative learning)

12. use critical thinking to perform tasks related to the Spanish language and Hispanic culture

Lección 10

After completing all material in this lesson, students should be able to:

1. talk about family

2. express uncertainty

3. tell someone what to do

4. express doubt

5. express emotion

6. state hopes

7. state an opinion

8. describe a household

9. discuss time

10. recognize the cultural connection between Bolivia, Colombia, Ecuador, Peru and Venezuela

11. respond with actions to commands and verbally to related questions (TPR)

12. engage in open-ended, personalized communication in pairs and small groups (cooperative learning)

13. use critical thinking to perform tasks related to the Spanish language and Hispanic culture

Lección 11

After completing all material in this lesson, students should be able to:

1. express events in the past

2. talk about the news

3. discuss what has happened

4. discuss a television broadcast

5. talk about everyday activities

6. describe people and objects

7. write about what someone has done

8. summarize cultural information on Uruguay

9. respond with actions to commands and verbally to related questions (TPR)

10. engage in open-ended, personalized communication in pairs and small groups (cooperative learning)

11. use critical thinking to perform tasks related to the Spanish language and Hispanic culture

Lección 12

After completing all material in this lesson, students should be able to:

1. talk about the news

2. identify sections of newspapers and magazines

3. relate two events in the past

4. express events in the past

5. discuss a radio broadcast

6. talk about soccer

7. add emphasis to a description

8. express wishes

9. write about what someone has done

10. summarize cultural information on Paraguay

11. recognize and use prefixes in Spanish

12. respond with actions to commands and verbally to related questions (TPR)

13. engage in open-ended, personalized communication in pairs and small groups (cooperative learning)

14. use critical thinking to perform tasks related to the Spanish language and Hispanic culture

Lección 13

After completing all material in this lesson, students should be able to:

1. seek and provide personal information

2. plan vacations

3. talk about the future

4. express emotion

5. talk about everyday activities

6. express uncertainty or probability

7. make travel and lodging arrangements

8. talk about the bullfight

9. summarize information about how to prepare a Spanish omelet

10. respond with actions to commands and verbally to related questions (TPR)

11. engage in open-ended, personalized communication in pairs and small groups (cooperative learning)

12. use critical thinking to perform tasks related to the Spanish language and Hispanic culture

Lección 14

After completing all material in this lesson, students should be able to:

1. identify people and items associated with travel

2. seek and provide personal information

3. state wishes and preferences

4. make travel and lodging arrangements

5. plan vacations

6. talk about schedules

7. use the twenty-four-hour clock

8. express logical conclusions

9. express uncertainty or probability

10. write about hopes and dreams

11. ummarize geographical information on Spain

12. discuss cultural diversity among the people of Spain

13. respond with actions to commands and verbally to related questions (TPR)

14. engage in open-ended, personalized communication in pairs and small groups (cooperative learning)

15. use critical thinking to perform tasks related to the Spanish language and Hispanic culture

Lección 15

After completing all material in this lesson, students should be able to:

1. discuss the future
2. express uncertainty
3. talk about hopes and dreams
4. seek and provide information about careers
5. express events in the past
6. relate two events in the past
7. express doubt
8. respond with actions to commands and verbally to related questions (TPR)
9. engage in open-ended, personalized communication in pairs and small groups (cooperative learning)
10. use critical thinking to perform tasks related to the Spanish language and Hispanic culture

Lección 16

After completing all material in this lesson, students should be able to:

1. discuss the future
2. talk about hopes and dreams
3. advise and suggest
4. state wishes and preferences
5. express doubt or uncertainty
6. express emotion
7. identify and locate some countries
8. write about the future
9. recognize and employ appropriate paralinguistic behavior for greetings and farewells
10. identify and locate some countries
11. respond with actions to commands and verbally to related questions (TPR)
12. engage in open-ended, personalized communication in pairs and small groups (cooperative learning)

13. use critical thinking to perform tasks related to the Spanish language and Hispanic culture

REVIEW LESSONS A - H

The following is a summary of the items included for activities that appear in the Review *(Repaso)* lesson:

Repaso A

1. talking about everyday activities
2. discussing personal grooming
3. seeking and providing personal information
4. talking about everyday activities
5. using definite articles with personal items
6. expressing past actions and events
7. stating when things are done
8. identifying items in a bathroom
9. pointing out and describing bathroom items in a store
10. using demonstrative pronouns
11. recognizing and identifying Hispanic influence in the United States
12. identifying parts of the body
13. discussing health
14. seeking and providing personal information
15. talking about everyday activities
16. discussing health
17. writing about everyday activities
18. self-test on common expressions
19. creative self-expression: *la vida diaria*

Repaso B

1. identifying places in the city
2. discussing what is sold in specific stores

Repaso C

11. identifying animals
12. using possessive adjectives
13. using possessive pronouns
14. self-test on common expressions
15. creative self-expression: *¿qué hacías?*

Repaso D

1. talking about what someone remembers
2. talking about what someone remembers
3. talking about everyday activities
4. identifying foods
5. *freír*
6. reporting past actions and events
7. reporting past actions and events
8. reading and ordering from a menu
9. Caribbean countries
10. reporting what was happening at a given time
11. adverbs ending in -*mente*
12. expressing length of time
13. self-test on common expressions
14. creative self-expression: ¿te acuerdas?

Repaso E

1. identifying verbs in the subjunctive
2. telling someone what not to do
3. talking about everyday activities
4. reporting what others say
5. telling someone what to do
6. South America
7. expressing emotion and doubt
8. expressing emotion
9. stating an opinion
10. expressing uncertainty about when something may happen

11. using adjectival clauses to describe
12. self-test on common expressions
13. creative self-expression: *hogar, dulce hogar*

Repaso F

1. talking about the news
2. discussing what has happened
3. expressing what has happened several times
4. expressing events in the past
5. talking about everyday activities
6. talking about a television broadcast
7. describing people and objects
8. identifying sections of newspapers and magazines
9. Uruguay and Paraguay
10. relating two events in the past
11. expressing events in the past
12. writing about what someone has done
13. self-test on common expressions
14. creative self-expression: *¿qué ha pasado?*

Repaso G

1. talking about the future
2. planning for the future
3. expressing uncertainty or probability
4. talking about the future
5. planning vacations
6. making travel arrangements
7. using the twenty-four-hour clock
8. Spain
9. telling what someone would do
10. expressing logical conclusions
11. planning vacations
12. expressing uncertainty or probability

13. self-test on common expressions

14. creative self-expression: *haciendo planes*

Repaso H

1. identifying jobs and careers

2. talking about peoples' careers

3. expressing doubt

4. expressing events in the past

5. talking about hopes and dreams

6. discussing the future

7. stating wishes and preferences

8. talking about hopes and dreams

9. identifying and locating some countries

10. countries and nationalities

11. self-test on common expressions

12. creative self-expression: *sueños y aspiraciones*

ADDITIONAL ACTIVITIES AND GAMES

Activities

The following activities can be used to enrich and supplement the presentation of new material in *Somos así 2*. Corresponding page numbers serve as a guide for using this section, although many listed activities can be adopted for use with different pages in the textbook or at other times during the school year. Three particular activities occur on a regular basis throughout these additional activities:

- *Lengua en acción* indicates activities that involve Total Physical Response (TPR). Whereas many teachers have used TPR, either extensively or on a limited basis, these activities often require an extra effort on the part of the teacher to prepare for and use TPR in the classroom. For this reason, numerous TPR activities have been included in the following pages to help the instructor to incorporate this effective learning technique into classroom activities on a regular basis. The activities will enhance student learning while relieving the teacher of the time required to prepare such material.

- *Interacción cooperativa* denotes an activity that is intended to offer students additional opportunities for cooperative learning beyond the textbook content. The activities require students to cooperate with one another in pairs or small groups using Spanish for authentic communication.

- *Creatividad mental* activities are designed to enhance the higher order thinking skills of the student. Educators have increasingly encouraged emphasis on critical thinking. The authors and publisher consider critical thinking an essential part of the total academic development of students. For this reason we have included a thorough and systematic program of higher order thinking skill activities that address comprehension, application, analysis, synthesis and evaluation along with many of the skills involved in each of these categories.

Page 2

Interacción cooperativa: Divide the class into groups of three and have three students practice introducing one another. One student introduces the other two, who must acknowledge the introduction correctly. Remember to have students shake hands when being introduced. The three then change roles until each person in the group has the opportunity to make an introduction and to acknowledge the introduction. After introductions are complete, students should tell about themselves and some of their interests, as Francisco does on page 2.

Additional activity: As a pre-listening activity, ask students to try to determine such things as how many people are speaking, whether the speakers are young or old, male or female. Ask if students hear questions or just statements. Then play the audiocassette as students listen with their books closed.

Page 3

Creatividad mental (comprehension—summarize): Have students prepare a list of ten cognates, listing the English equivalent of words next to the Spanish.

Creatividad mental (application—produce): Ask several students to say something they do not like to do.

Page 16

Interacción cooperativa: Have students prepare their family trees. Allow them to make up any of the information they wish. Then, working in pairs, have students take turns asking questions in order to try to duplicate each other's family tree.

Page 19

Lengua en acción: Write in random order on the chalkboard several numbers between 0-59. Then call on individual students saying, for example: (name), *ve a la pizarra. Toca el número....* (Watch as several students touch two or three numbers each.); (name), *ve a la pizarra. Borra el número....* (Have each student erase two or three numbers.); (name), *ve a la pizarra. Escribe el número....* (Each student writes two or three numbers.). Doing this activity in the order given will focus student attention on both receptive (listening and reading) and productive (writing) skills. Extend the activity by having students read aloud some of the commands while their classmates respond.

Page 20

Additional activity: Hold up a card with a number on it while saying a number, and have your students say aloud the words *sí* or *no* to indicate if you are holding up the number you have said.

Additional activity: Have students practice writing the numbers as you read them out loud.

Additional activity: Play a game of Bingo, practicing the numbers 0-75.

Additional activity: Help students practice the numbers by having them count around the class, each person giving one number. Go front to back, back to front or across the rows. When students are

comfortable with numbers, use the same technique to have them count by 5's, 3's, 2's. You may also wish to have students count off in order numbers containing a 3 (for example 3, 13, 23).

Additional activity: Try holding up a card with a number on it while saying a number, and have your students say out loud the words *sí* or *no* to indicate if you are holding up the number you have said. As a variation, call on students to identify the number orally in Spanish, or have a student go to the blackboard and write the numeral you are holding.

Page 21

Creatividad mental (acquisition—match): Have students write special dates on one set of index cards along with what the special occasion is on another set of cards. Shuffle the cards. Then have the students match the date and occasion.

Page 22

Additional activity: Say several years (i.e., 2000) in Spanish while students write them down. Maintain a rapid pace so students do not have idle time. Have students exchange papers and check each other's spelling.

Additional activity: As an alternative, give the years in Spanish quickly while students write the numeral that represents each year *(2000 = dos mil)*.

Page 24

Interacción cooperativa: After students have worked on activity 12, have them work in pairs writing their actual schedules (help them with Spanish words for subjects they take). They should exchange schedules and ask *¿A qué hora es tu clase de...?* (Since A has B's schedule, A can verify if B answers correctly.) Point out the use of *tu clase* rather than *la clase*. Students should take turns asking and answering questions about their schedules until all subjects on each schedule have been included.

Page 30

Practice the comparatives and superlatives with simple illustrations such as one person labeled with a name, a dollar symbol and an amount, another person labeled with a name and the same amount and a third labeled with a name and a higher amount: *Pilar, $200 pesos; Carlos, $200 pesos; Andrés, $500 pesos.* Then hold up pictures of Pilar and Andrés and say, *Pilar tiene 200 pesos y Andrés tiene 500 pesos. Pilar tiene menos pesos que Andrés. Andrés tiene más pesos que Pilar. ¿Quién tiene menos pesos?* (Ask a student to respond.) Continue with *¿Quién tiene más pesos?* (Ask for a response.) Next ask a student to describe Pilar in relation to Andrés: *Tiene menos pesos que Andrés.* Ask a student to describe Andrés in relation to Pilar: *Tiene más pesos que Pilar.* Hold up pictures of Pilar and Carlos while making statements and asking questions to elicit responses: *...tiene tanto dinero como...* and *...tiene tantas pesos como....* In similar fashion use three illustrations of persons with an item that may be described as larger or smaller, for example, and ask questions for responses that include the following: *más grande que, menos grande que, más pequeño que, menos pequeño que, tan grande como, tan pequeño como.*

Lengua en acción: Have students prepare two columns of names for imaginary people, placing a number next to each name to indicate how much money each person has. Then working in pairs, have the students make statements comparing how much the named people have. Students should point at the name of the person who corresponds to each statement their partner makes. For example, *¿Quién tiene más dinero, Pablo o María?* Circulate to keep students on task and to offer assistance. You may wish to contribute to some of the conversations by stopping for a moment and asking or answering a question or two for each pair of students.

Page 52

Interacción cooperativa: After completing the presentation of the dialog (playing the audiocassette, modeling words and phrases for student repetition, covering the activity items), have students work in threes practicing the dialog. Circulate and assist with pronunciation and intonation.

Page 54

Interacción cooperativa: As an extension of activity 2, and as a review of classroom vocabulary, have students work in pairs asking one another about objects they do or do not see in the classroom. Students should take turns asking if the classmate sees a particular item. The classmate must answer, using *sí* or *no* and the appropriate direct object pronoun: *¿Ves la pizarra?/Sí, (No, no) la veo.*

Page 62

Additional activity: Have students research a particular aspect of your community that is Hispanic in origin.

Page 64

Creatividad mental (synthesis—associate): Have students prepare a list of geographical sites, businesses, etc., in your community that have names in Spanish.

Page 79

Additional activity: Practice the demonstrative pronouns and review the demonstrative and possessive adjectives by asking questions containing a classroom object. Students must answer the questions, using an appropriate demonstrative pronoun adjective: *¿De quién es ese libro?/Este es mi libro. Ese es el libro de Juan. Aquel libro es su libro* (pointing to another student).

Page 83

Additional activity: Model each word or expression and have students repeat. Then ask students to use the word or expression in a sentence. This activity would be appropriate for all lists of vocabulary found in *Somos así 2.*

Additional activity: *El verdugo.* The idea of the game is to guess a word. One student goes to the board and writes one blank for each letter of any word. The other students then begin to guess letters of the alphabet that might be in that word, Each correct letter is inserted into the proper blank. If the correct letter is guessed, the student at the board draws in a part of a hanged man. The game continues until the word had been guessed or the complete hanged man has been drawn. You may want to make the game more challenging by drawing in a part of the hanged man for every vowel guessed, since the vowels first would probably make the entire word much easier to figure out. This game may be played with the class divided into two teams or with the entire class guessing the letters.

Page 90

Lengua en acción: Try using TPR to teach and reinforce the parts of the body. Teach the following commands, combining them with the appropriate parts of the body: *toca, mueve, rasca, tira, levanta, baja, abre, cierra.* Parts of the body you may wish to include are: *el brazo, la cabeza, el dedo, la mano, el pie, la pierna, la boca, la cara, el codo, el cuello, el diente, el estómago, la garganta, el hombro, la lengua, la muñeca, la nariz, el ojo, la oreja, el pecho, el pelo, la rodilla, el tobillo.* You can review the present progressive by asking individual students questions after each command: (name), *¿qué estás tocando?;* (name), *¿qué está tocando* (second student's name)?

Page 102

Additional activity: Try using the *A escribir* section as a quiz on writing, as a replacement or in addition to the end-of-lesson summative testing of writing skills or for prescriptive testing in order to provide remediation.

Page 103

Additional activity: Ask students to say a word they have learned in Spanish and then select someone else to spell the word. Have them check their spelling and then switch roles.

Vocabulary review: Dictate a letter of the alphabet to the class. Give students three minutes to write any words they can think of in Spanish which begin with that letter. After calling time, ask students to read their lists aloud. The student with the longest list of correct words wins.

Page 104

Additional activity: Prepare students for the content of a reading by asking some general questions on the reading topic, such as the questions found in the *Preparación*. Next, play the first paragraph of the recording of the *Lectura*, using the corresponding audiocassette that is part of the Audiocassette Program. As an alternative, you may choose to read the first paragraph yourself. Read the paragraph again with students following along in the book. Give students a moment to look over the paragraph silently on their own and then have them ask questions. Ask for a student to volunteer to read the paragraph aloud. Continue in this way for subsequent paragraphs.

Page 122

Lengua en acción: Use the *tú* forms of a few verbs for the following TPR activity. Select several students to react to the informal commands of the corresponding verbs: *Abre el libro; Cierra el libro; Toca el libro.* Work with one verb several times before going to another verb. To avoid monotony, vary the commands slightly: (student's name), *abre el libro;* (student's name), *abre el cuaderno.* Perform the action or use gestures only if a student does not respond.

Page 128

Additional activity: Take students on a field trip to a restaurant that serves some of the foods mentioned in the *A propósito* entitled *Las comidas nacionales.* Consider requiring that students speak only Spanish during the trip.

Page 130

Practice with the *Uds.* forms of the commands by having the entire class perform certain actions or gestures as you read them aloud in Spanish. The commands should be presented in as many logical pairs as possible *(abran, cierren; escriban, borren; escuchen, repitan).* Practice the action or gesture two or three times with students, then repeat the pair of commands one or two times with no actions or gestures.

Page 141

Interacción cooperativa: Have students prepare a map that shows the route between two places, such as school and the student's home. Then, working in pairs, have students take turns explaining the directions to a classmate.

Page 142

Additional activity: Have students research a particular aspect about Mexico and write a report on what they find out. As an alternative, have students present their findings to the class.

Page 157

Additional activity: Encourage students to learn to become good listeners by asking follow-up questions about general content: What are the speakers talking about? Are they angry with each other? Did students notice any names in the dialog? Play the audiocassette again with books open, having students read along silently. Ask students to point out items unlike English (punctuation—¿ and ¡—and accents). Have students repeat after you as you read the content in short phrases. You may choose to act out or paraphrase the meanings of words and expressions, avoiding word-for-word translations (for instance, for *cinturones de seguridad,* act like you are buckling the seat belt in a car or plane, and so forth).

Page 174

Additional activity: For a change of pace, use any of the photos or illustrations in the textbook, and ask students to describe what they see or to make up a story about what they see.

Page 175

Additional activity: After sufficient practice, have several pairs of students present their dialogs in front of the class.

Page 190

Creatividad mental (comprehension—identify): Use the map transparencies to practice the adjectives of nationality for the Spanish-speaking parts of the world. Say the following while pointing to one of the countries on a map transparency: *Si* (name of person/people) *es de aquí, ¿qué es?*; students should answer with *Es* (nationality). (You may choose to have various students direct the class to add variety.)

Additional activity: For additional writing practice, and in order to encourage visual learners with artistic skills, have students prepare maps of the Spanish-speaking world in Spanish, adding any details they wish to borrow from the color maps at the beginning of the textbook. Where students write the name of the country, have them add in parentheses the adjective(s) of nationality that identifies someone from that country.

Page 192

Additional activity: *¿Dónde estaban?* In order to review the verb *estar*, have students bring in cutouts from magazines of members of various places throughout the world (preferably places where Spanish is spoken). Then have them write captions below the pictures telling about who was in each and where the people were, using the appropriate present-tense form of *estar* and each of the subject pronouns. After they complete the written assignment you may wish to have students work in pairs, asking one another about the photographs or presenting the information to the class: *Aquí están mis tíos, en San Salvador.*

Creatividad mental (application—demonstrating; evaluation—supporting): Write several phrases on the board that are preceded by *ser (de San Salvador, inteligente, las 8:00)* and several that are preceded by *estar (bien, regular, en Honduras, en la clase)*. Point to a word or phrase and ask *¿Ser o estar?* After students respond, ask *¿Por qué?* and call on one student to support the answer. (The response may be in English unless you prefer to give students the Spanish words *origen, característica, condición* and *lugar*.)

Page 208

Additional activity: Prepare a bulletin board that shows pictures of the animals students are learning in *Capítulo 3*. If you do not label the bulletin board with the animals' names, you can use the pictures as an oral review during class, when appropriate. If you decide to label the animals, the bulletin board will serve as a constant review that students will see before them during the time you leave the display up. As an alternative, have students prepare the bulletin board display.

Page 239

Creatividad mental (comprehension—convert): Have students convert several metric measurements as a class activity. (You may wish to obtain the help of a math or home economics teacher.) As an alternative, take student suggestions to prepare a list of several measurements that students will convert as a homework assignment.

Page 243

Interacción cooperativa: Working in pairs, have students take turns asking one another what foods they like on the menu for the restaurant *La Buena Mesa.*

Page 277

Interacción cooperativa: Working in pairs, have students talk about the chores that are reviewed in the *A propósito* entitled *¿Qué recuerdas?* Suggest that they talk about who does the indicated chores, how the student feels about doing each activity, etc.

Page 289

Interacción cooperativa: Have students bring in magazine pictures of four activities they like and four they do not like. They should look up any new vocabulary and learn new words, as appropriate. Ask students to work in pairs to do the following: First, they should teach each other the new vocabulary; then, students should take turns asking each other which activities or objects they like, asking *¿Te gusta...?* When all students have completed their interviews, select several students to report on the likes and dislikes of the interview partner while holding up and showing the appropriate picture: *A* (name) *(no) le gusta....*

Page 307

Additional activity: Have students write five rules to live by, using five different impersonal expressions and the present tense of the subjunctive: *Es importante que yo siga las reglas de la casa.*

Page 319

Creatividad mental (evaluation—concluding, appraising, comparing): Discuss student conclusions about Hispanic culture based upon the *Lectura* entitled *La familia hispana.* Ask how students feel about what Mimi, Eva, Marta, Olman and Alejandro say about their families and how family life in the United States compares to family life in these Spanish-speaking natives' homes.

Page 337

Interacción cooperativa: Have students work in pairs to practice asking and answering questions using the *tú* and *yo* forms of several verbs in the past perfect tense (make sure they use the rising intonation of questions). Student A could ask *¿Has comido hoy?, ¿Has visto alguna película nueva?,* and so forth. Student B should respond affirmatively to each question. After all verbs have been covered, Student A again asks the questions and Student B responds negatively *(No, he comido hoy).* Then have students change roles.

Page 371

Lengua en acción: Use a wall map of South America or an overhead transparency of the map in the front of this book to review Uruguay and Paraguay. Have individual students go to the map *(Ve or Camina al mapa).* Have students touch *(toca)* or point to *(señala)* the items mentioned in activity 9: *su capital es Asunción, el río Paraguay divide al país en dos regiones naturales,* and so forth.

Page 378

Talk with your colleagues in home economics or with the staff of your school cafeteria to see if arrangements can be made for your class to make this recipe during school hours. As an alternative, have several students make the recipe at home. Students can either bring in the *tortilla española* for everyone to sample or prepare the dish for a family meal.

Page 389

Lengua en acción: Check students' understanding of verb tense by making several travel statements that have either already occurred or that will occur: *Fui a España el año pasado./Mi familia y yo iremos a la América del Sur el año que viene.* Have students raise their left hand if the sentence is in the past tense; have them raise their right hand if the sentence is in the future tense.

Page 395

Additional activity: Spot-check students' understanding of the twenty-four-hour clock. Put several times on the board. Be sure to use the twenty-four-hour clock for several times *(12:30, 17:50,* etc.). Then call on students and ask *¿Qué hora es?,* as you point to the time.

Page 398

Creatividad mental (analysis—compare and contrast): Say the future tense of several verbs and call on students to give the conditional tense of each.

Page 405

Additional activity: Divide the class into groups of two. Each group prepares a conversation in Spanish between a hotel room clerk and a tourist who wants a room. Instruct students to use as many new words and expressions as possible.

Page 427

Lengua en acción: Ask students to turn to the illustration of various people's jobs. Inform students that you will be saying several words in Spanish. Have students raise their right hand if the item they hear appears in the illustration; they are to raise their left hand if the word does not appear in the illustration.

Page 428

Lengua en acción: (Use variations of this TPR activity to teach or review any vocabulary topic.) Choose a theme, "jobs," for example. Inform students they are to raise their right hand if the item names a job; they must raise their left hand if the item does not name a job. (This part of the activity will vary depending upon the vocabulary topic.) Then say several words in Spanish to teach and test student comprehension of vocabulary: *el mesero* (right hand), *la zanahoria* (left hand), *la mujer de negocios* (right hand), *el cuchillo* (left hand), *el avión* (left hand), and so forth.

Page 437

Lead a class discussion on students' feelings about the role that family will play in their futures. First, ask what students think about Carlos' letter. Do they agree that having a strong and united family is the most important thing in their futures? What would be the ideal age to begin a family? Then, ask if students believe having a family will interfere with having a career.

Page 445

Critical thinking (analysis—compare and contrast): Lead a discussion comparing and contrasting the use of gestures and body posture for communicating shown here with the gestures and body posture that students are familiar with in their own culture for nonspoken communication.

Page 454

Additional activity: For additional writing practice, and in order to encourage visual learners with artistic skills, have students prepare maps of the world in Spanish, adding any details they wish.

Creatividad mental (application—demonstrating): Provide students with blank map outlines of the world (or have students prepare the maps) on which they can write the names of the countries and capitals they know.

Creatividad mental (analysis—categorizing): Provide students with a list of countries and capitals. Then have them match the capitals to the appropriate countries.

Creatividad mental (synthesis—combining and associating; evaluation—justifying): Write several words on the board or on an overhead transparency (i.e., *periódico, España, maletas, Colombia*). Ask students to write or say words that are related to the words you wrote down (they should be ready to justify their answers in English): *periódico, revista* (both can be read); *España, paella* (*paella* is a saffron-flavored rice dish that is very popular in Spain). As an alternative, have students do the activity in pairs.

Games

Games, mnemonic devices and similar activities are excellent educational tools, giving students the opportunity to learn in a context that varies the daily routine. All games and activities can be modified to suit the needs of your students or to support your particular approach to teaching.

Lotería: Using a commercially produced Bingo set, call the numbers in Spanish. Since most Bingo sets go only up through the number 75, you might want to make your own set of numbers to call so that numbers through 100 can be included. In this case, the students need to make their own cards, placing numbers 1-20 in the first column, 21 through 40 in the second column and so on.

Lotería can also be played with verb forms or vocabulary. Make a master list of seventy-five verb forms (present tense forms of twenty-five different verbs) and use the Bingo-calling tokens to call out the verb form found in the I-21 blank, for example. (Use a sheet with seventy-five spaces, "B-1 through B-15, I-16 through I-30, N-31 through N-45, G-46 through G-60 and O-61 through O-75," and fill in each blank with one verb form in any order. The numbered tokens from the Bingo set are then used to determine which verb form will be called.) Students will fill in a blank Bingo (*Lotería*) form with whatever verb form they wish from the list given, and have to cover five in a row in order to win. To make the game more challenging, call the verb forms in English so that students have to know the meanings of the forms they write in. When a student wins, he or she must call out the forms covered in Spanish. Commercially produced games of *Lotería* are also available. However, you can use any group of 75 words for this activity by having students make their own *Lotería* cards.

Buzz (numbers): Select a word (*¡Caramba!, ¡Olé!* or any other) and choose a number between one and ten. Have the students begin counting, one number per student. Whenever the chosen number, or a multiple of the number is reached, the student whose turn it is must say the word you selected instead of the number. If the student forgets, he or she must drop out of the game.

Streetcar (vocabulary review): Prepare file cards with the words you want to practice in Spanish on one side (it may be helpful to indicate infinitives with an asterisk and include articles with nouns) and in English on the reverse side. You may extend this game by using synonyms and antonyms. Your list could develop from the active vocabulary words listed at the end of each lesson. Decide whether you want the students to produce the English or the Spanish. Students should study the vocabulary before playing Streetcar.

The object of this game is to get all the way back to one's seat. The teacher may direct this game or have a student do it.

Begin on the left side of class with the first row. The first student stands up next to the second, who remains seated. Show a card to these students while saying the word. The first of the two students who responds correctly moves on to compete with the third student.

Whoever answers correctly stands next to the third student; for example, if the second student wins the round he or she moves on to the third student, and the first student sits down in the second student's seat. If neither of the first two students can answer after five seconds, the third student is given an opportunity to respond. If there is still no answer, use the card as a free review, ask the class to define the problem word and choose a new card. This should be a relatively fast-paced game. By saying the target word as you show it, students practice assigning sound to visual cues as well.

Rhythm/Concentration (verbs): This game can be used for practicing the numbers or for reviewing or practicing verbs. The same rhythm is maintained: students tap the tops of their desks twice, clap their hands twice and snap their fingers twice—words may be called out only during the snapping of fingers.

For practice on the imperfect tense of verbs, for example, the first student in each row gives a verb infinitive (*hablar*) on the first snapping of fingers, the next student gives a subject pronoun (*tú*) on the second and the third student must respond with the appropriate answer (*tú hablabas*) on the third snapping of fingers. Students who make an error move to the end of the row and the other students move up. Try to have an uneven number of students in each row so that every student will have the opportunity to match subject pronoun and verb ending. All the students in each row monitor each other for errors. You also may have the entire class participate rather than play the game by rows. In this case you may want to point to students for verb infinitive, subject pronoun and response.

Killer (grammar, culture, etc.): This is a team game. Divide the class into two or three teams. If the class is large you may wish to have four teams, with two selected teams beginning the competition and the other two observing. The winning team then competes with the third team and the winner of this round competes with the final team. Have the two competing teams seated in front of the board, with a line dividing the board for the written responses for each team. It may be useful to ask one student to keep a time clock, stopping the action at thirty seconds (or fewer, if you choose). The first person on each team is given a piece of chalk. For verb practice, for example, prepare a list of verbs in advance. Clarify the topic area for students (present indicative of irregular verbs, for example). At the signal from the timekeeper, give one of the verbs and then cue with a subject pronoun. As a variation you may wish to give the English (she has gone) while students write the Spanish equivalent *(ella ha ido)*. This variation should be used, obviously, at another time rather than combined with the verb/subject pronoun version. After the Spanish or English prompt is given, students with the chalk leave their seats and write the response on the board. The first student to write the correct response receives a point for that team. The chalk is then passed on to the next team member. The chalk may also be passed to the next team member if a student does not know or is unsure of the correct response. If neither team can answer correctly within the time limit, go to another item.

You may also use Killer to review cultural information, preparing a list of questions in advance that require short answers (two or three words, or a short phrase). Your questions and the responses may be in English or Spanish, depending on your students and the material that you wish to cover.

Jeopardy (general review): This game is especially good as a review before the midyear or final exam, but it can be used at almost any time in many different ways. Similar to the television game show, write a series of categories horizontally on the board (to review *Capítulo 3*, for example: animal names, animal sounds, El Salvador, Honduras, nationalities, imperfect tense of verbs, use of *ser* vs. *estar*, vocabulary, position of adjectives, showing possession). Write the numbers ten through fifty by tens under each category. Prepare questions in advance; unlike the television game show, students need not respond with a question. Questions may be completions, synonyms or antonyms, translations, direct questions, matching, and so forth. Divide the class into three or four teams and tell students that each of them have an imaginary buzzer which they must use if they wish to participate.

To see which team will go first, ask a question that may be answered by any student. The first student who sounds the buzzer gets a chance to answer. The team that correctly answers the opening question has the opportunity to choose a category and a dollar amount. Read the question, allowing that team to respond within a time limit (ten or fifteen seconds). If not answered within the specified time limit, the question is open to the entire class, but buzzers must be used; that is, students should not randomly blurt out answers.

Prepare several Daily Double questions, as well. Use these when enthusiasm for the game wanes. Whatever the dollar amount in the chosen category is at that moment, double it. These questions may be answered by any team, not just the team that chose the category. Note: If you wish to practice numbers while playing the game, the dollar amounts may be given in odd numbers.

When a question is answered correctly, write the answer in the space left by the erased dollar amount as you keep score. This will provide students with visual reinforcement of the material. When the entire board is filled with answers, total the scores. You may wish to offer prizes as an incentive.

Susurrando (commands): Make up teams of about five students each. Have a list already prepared of ten commands. Make enough copies of this list for the number of teams that you will have, then cut each list into ten pieces, separating the commands. Have each team stand in columns around you like the spokes of a wheel with about three feet between each student. Then ask the first member of each team to stand in a close circle around you, hand them the first command and whisper it to them so that they have the correct pronunciation. No one else in the room should be able to hear you. Those students then whisper the same command to the second person in their lines, making sure that no one can see the sentence. The second person turns around and whispers it to the third and so on. The last person from each team must come up to you and perform the command as it is understood. After each has performed the command, you may want to have students (except for team leaders who received the written command) guess the original command, especially if the commands as performed differ greatly from the original. You also may want to make this a contest by awarding points to the team that guesses and correctly states the original command.

As a variation, you may give each team a different command so that there will be more variety in the commands performed. Again, you may wish to make it a contest by awarding points to the team that guesses and correctly states the original command for their team or for any other team. After the first command (or group of commands if you give different commands to each team), the first student on each team moves to the back of the column and the second student in each group receives the next command(s) from you.

Stop-the-Clock (vocabulary review): Make up a series of small cards with pictures on one side and their Spanish definition on the other and distribute them to the class. Divide the class into two groups and choose one person to be *It* for each group (you will have two games going at once). The rest of the students sit on their desks (or stand in from of them) in a circle, holding their cards with the picture facing out. The person who is *It* stands in the center.

To begin the game, pick one student in each group. Those students must say the name in Spanish of the pictures on the cards they are holding and the name of the picture on another student's card. (It makes it harder on the person who is *It* to not be looking at the person whose card is named. Thus, you may wish to advise students to name a second card that is to the side or behind *It*.) The person in the center of the circle must find the second person and point at the corresponding picture, thus "stopping the clock," before the second student can name both his or her picture and another person's picture. Make sure the person in the center is accurately pointing at or preferably touching the picture. If someone's clock is stopped, that person is then *It*.

¿Dónde está? (directional vocabulary and commands): Choose a small object such as a piece of chalk, show it to the students and ask them to hide it somewhere in the room. Go out of the room for a few minutes while they hide the item. When you return they will help you find it by giving you directional commands or indicating direction (*Doble a la derecha, está cerca, mire arriba,* etc.).

Next divide the class into groups of four or five, choose one person from each group to leave the room and repeat the game, this time with familiar commands.

El Detective (general review): This game may be played with a number of different objectives: to help students get to know one another, to practice specific vocabulary, to practice different verb tenses, and so forth. Make a number of lists with five to ten different items on each list. If the object is for students to get to know each other, include items such as *le gusta el fútbol, el béisbol,* etc. (a different sport on each list); *come pollo, ensalada, hamburguesas,* etc. (a different food on each list); *mañana va a la playa, al concierto, al cine,* etc. (a different place on each list); and so forth. It is fun to include an unusual category to make the activity more interesting. Copy the lists to equal the number of students you have so that each group (of five, for example) has the same list and different groups have different lists. *El detective* must fill in his or her list by asking fellow students if certain categories apply to them and if so, they sign the list by the appropriate category. Students will practice the *tú* form while asking classmates questions (*¿Te gusta el fútbol?*), and may practice third-person singular by reporting the findings to the class after all students have completed the activity.

CLASSROOM EXPRESSIONS

Begin to use some Spanish in the classroom from the first day of class and continue to use it increasingly on subsequent days throughout the year. While this may seem difficult for some teachers, the model lesson plan included in the introduction to the Teacher's Edition offers guidelines for teaching (TPR activities, games, and so forth) that will make using Spanish not only possible but quite simple as well. Furthermore, annotations throughout the Teacher's Edition of the textbook will assist teachers in using Spanish in class frequently.

For students who are having difficulty with the notion of using Spanish as the primary means of communication, explain that you will paraphrase, use gestures or act out expressions in order to avoid an excessive use of English. Setting this tone will help students become more aware of their need to use the target language. You may choose, however, to note that important points such as homework assignments, grammar items, and so on, will be given or repeated in English if necessary.

As students become accustomed to hearing and using Spanish their aural comprehension will improve and they will develop increased confidence and comfort. You also may ease student trepidations about hearing Spanish by indicating that it is not necessary to understand every word. Inform students that learning a language involves a lot of educated and intelligent guessing and listening for key words rather than trying to understand or look up every unknown word they encounter.

Encourage students to respond to directions in Spanish and to give answers in Spanish as well. Initially they may feel frustrated that their ability to use Spanish is not on a par with their ability to use English, so you may need to explain that people often use one-word answers and incomplete phrases to communicate in their native language. (Give some examples in English for comparison purposes.) Point out that the more students use Spanish, the more natural it will become as a means of communication.

The following are some useful expressions that you may wish to introduce to students early in the year:

Abre (Abran Uds.) el libro/cuaderno en la página....   Open your book/workbook to page....

Acuérdate (Acuérdense Uds.) de (+ verb)....   Remember to....

Apunta/Señala (Apunten Uds./ Señalen Uds.)....	Point at....
Borra (Borren Uds.) la pizarra.	Erase the chalkboard.
Cállate (Cállense Uds.).	Be quiet.
Cierra (Cierren Uds.) el libro/cuaderno.	Close your book/notebook.
Contesta/Responde (Contesten Uds./ Responden Uds.).	Answer.
Continúa/Sigue (Continúen Uds./ Sigan Uds.).	Continue.
Copia (Copien Uds.)....	Copy....
Da (Den Uds.) la vuelta.	Turn around.
Dibuja (Dibujen Uds.)....	Draw....
Dime (Díganme Uds.)....	Tell me....
Empieza (Empiecen Uds.) ahora.	Begin now.
Escoge (Escojan Uds.)....	Choose....
Entrégame (Entréguenme Uds.) la tarea.	Hand in your homework to me.
Escribe (Escriban Uds.)....	Write....
Escucha (Escuchen Uds.).	Listen.
Estudia (Estudien Uds.)....	Study....
Formen Uds. grupos de....	Form groups of....
Habla (Hablen Uds.) en español.	Speak in Spanish.
Levanta (Levanten Uds.) la mano (para contestar).	Raise your hand (to answer).
Lee (Lean Uds.)...en voz alta.	Read...out loud.
Levántate (Levántense Uds.).	Stand up.
Llévate (Llévense Uds.)....	Take...with you.
Mira (Miren Uds.).	Look.
Oye (Oigan Uds.).	Listen.
Para (Paren Uds.).	Stop.
Pasa (Pasen Uds.) a la pizarra.	Go to the chalkboard.
Piensa (Piensen Uds.).	Think.
Pon (Pongan Uds.)....	Put/Place....
Presta (Presten Uds.) atención a....	Pay attention to....
Pronuncia (Pronuncien Uds.)....	Pronounce....

Recoge (Recojan Uds.)....	Pick up....
Recuerda (Recuerden Uds.)....	Remember....
Repite (Repitan Uds.).	Repeat.
Revisa (Revisen Uds.)....	Review....
Quita (Quiten Uds.) todo de encima de sus pupitres.	Take everything off the top of your desks.
Saca (Saquen Uds.) una hoja de papel/un bolígrafo/un lápiz.	Take out a sheet of paper/a pen/a pencil.
Siéntate (Siéntense Uds.).	Sit down.
Toca (Toquen Uds.)....	Touch....
Trabajen Uds. en parejas en....	Work in pairs on....
Trae (Traigan Uds.)....	Bring....
Trata (Traten Uds.).	Try.
Ve (Vayan Uds.) a....	Go to....
Ven (Vengan Uds.) aquí.	Come here.
Muy bien.	Very good.
Excelente.	Excellent.
Para mañana....	For tomorrow....
Una vez más.	One more time.
Más alto/bajo.	Louder/Softer.
Silencio.	Quiet.
Otra vez.	Once more.
Vamos a tener una prueba/un examen.	We're going to have a quiz/a test.
¿Quién sabe (la respuesta)?	Who knows (the answer)?
¿Alguien?	Anyone?
Todos juntos.	All together.
En español.	In Spanish.
¿Hay preguntas?	Are there any questions?
¿Cómo se dice...(en español)?	How do you say...(in Spanish)?
¿Cómo se escribe...?	How do you write...?
¿Qué quiere decir...?	What does...mean?
No sé.	I don't know.
No comprendo/entiendo.	I don't understand.
No recuerdo.	I don't remember.

Tengo una pregunta.	I have a question.
Bueno, pues, este...	Okay (Well, Um)....
Yo creo/pienso que....	I believe/think that....
la palabra	the word
la respuesta	the answer
la frase	the sentence
la línea	the line
el número	the number